College English
Self-adaptive Reading

新指南大学英语
自主阅读 ②

总主编　李华东
主　编　刘瑾玉
副主编　陈　颖　赵玲玲　王伟禄
编　者　孔令宇　阿斯罕　高友晗
　　　　阿荣娜　刘慧丹

清华大学出版社
北京

内容简介

《新指南大学英语自主阅读》1—4册是根据教育部最新发布的《大学英语教学指南（2020版）》，为我国普通高等院校大学生量身打造的一套自主阅读教材。

本套书每册包括8个单元，每个单元包含视频导入、语言输入、阅读技巧和语言输出4大部分：导入部分精选主题相关视频，扫码即看，并设计有理解性和思辨性练习；语言输入部分由Banked Cloze、Long Passage和Short Passages 3个板块组成，所选篇章均借助语言数据技术，标注了篇章长度（NW）、语言难度（GL）、语言学术性（AWL percentage）和关键词（Keywords）等数据，练习与大学英语四、六级考试题型完全接轨；1—4册共32个单元的阅读技巧板块有机融入，构成完整的阅读技能训练体系；语言输出部分聚焦学术词汇训练和写作训练。

本套教材兼顾基础级别目标（第1、2册）和提高级别目标（第3、4册），适合我国普通高校一、二年级大学生使用。

版权所有，侵权必究。举报：010-62782989，beiqinquan@tup.tsinghua.edu.cn。

图书在版编目（CIP）数据

新指南大学英语自主阅读. 2 / 李华东总主编；刘瑾玉主编. — 北京：清华大学出版社，2021.8（2024.8重印）
　ISBN 978-7-302-58495-7

Ⅰ. ①新… Ⅱ. ①李… ②刘… Ⅲ. ①英语—阅读教学—高等学校—教材 Ⅳ. ①H319.4

中国版本图书馆CIP数据核字(2021)第121305号

责任编辑：刘细珍
封面设计：子　一
责任校对：王凤芝
责任印制：丛怀宇

出版发行：清华大学出版社
　　　　网　　址：https://www.tup.com.cn, https://www.wqxuetang.com
　　　　地　　址：北京清华大学学研大厦A座　　邮　编：100084
　　　　社 总 机：010-83470000　　邮　购：010-62786544
　　　　投稿与读者服务：010-62776969, c-service@tup.tsinghua.edu.cn
　　　　质量反馈：010-62772015, zhiliang@tup.tsinghua.edu.cn
印 装 者：大厂回族自治县彩虹印刷有限公司
经　　销：全国新华书店
开　　本：185mm×260mm　　印　张：12　　字　数：220千字
版　　次：2021年8月第1版　　印　次：2024年8月第6次印刷
定　　价：58.00元

产品编号：092135-02

前言

《新指南大学英语自主阅读》是根据教育部最新发布的《大学英语教学指南（2020版）》（以下简称"《指南》"），借助语言数据技术，为我国普通高等院校大学生量身定制的一套自主阅读教材。

一、教材特色

本套教材务求体现以下特色：

1. 依据《指南》编写，针对基础和提高级别

《指南》指出，"大学英语教学目标分为基础、提高、发展三个级别"，并对三个级别的阅读理解能力进行了描述。本套教材针对基础和提高两个级别研发，能覆盖绝大多数普通高等院校大学生，满足他们提高英语阅读理解能力的需求。

2. 借助语言数据技术，助力自主阅读

为帮助学习者了解自己的水平，掌控自己的阅读进度，本套教材所选阅读篇章均标注了篇章语言数据，具体如下：

- 篇章长度（number of words，简称"NW"）：便于自学者了解自己的阅读速度（速度＝篇章长度/阅读时间）。

- 语言难度（Flesch-Kincaid Grade Level，简称"GL"）：GL数值等于美国学生年级，比如GL为8的篇章从难度上适合美国八年级学生阅读。近10年来我国主要英语考试的英语阅读篇章GL数值分别为：高考英语8.3左右，大学英语四级考试10.8左右，大学英语六级考试11.8左右。

- 语言学术性（Academic Word List percentage，简称"AWL percentage"）：采用Coxhead于2000年研发的学术词表，计算每篇阅读中学术词汇比例，便于自学者提高自身学术英语阅读能力。依据Coxhead的研究，学术语篇的AWL percentage比例为9.9%左右。

- 关键词（keywords）：每篇文章提供3个关键词，便于自学者在阅读前大致了解文章内容。

按照克拉申（Krashen）的输入假设（Input Hypothesis），制约语言习得的

主要因素是语言输入,而最佳的语言输入是稍稍超出学习者现有语言能力的输入。借助上述语言数据,自学者可以了解自己的阅读水平和阅读喜好,从而选择稍稍超出自己现有阅读水平的篇章进行阅读,进而有针对性地提高自己的语言能力。

3. 实施主题教学模式,提高词汇复现率

本套教材选择与中国大学生学习和生活密切相关的话题,每个单元围绕同一个话题展开,在加大学习者知识广度和深度的同时,提高词汇复现率,并穿插视频观看(Viewing)和写作(Writing)环节,有效将学生的认知性词汇(passive vocabulary)转化为复用式词汇(active vocabulary)。

二、教材架构

本套教材包括 4 册书,书后均附视频脚本和练习参考答案。每册主题和语言技能安排如下表:

级别	主题	阅读技能设置
1	大学生活、教育、时尚、饮食、情感、旅行、性格、社交	以《指南》规定的**基础**级别目标阅读技能为主
2	爱情、成长、大学校园文化、生活方式、感情与交往、合作与冲突、创业、职业规划	
3	课外生活、语言的力量、健康与美容、跨文化交际、数据时代、创新、人工智能、基因技术	以《指南》规定的**提高**级别目标阅读技能为主
4	职业规划、工作选择、财务管理、旅行、环保、因特网与生活、工作地点选择、新教育模式	

三、单元设置

本套教材每册包括 8 个单元,每个单元包含 4 大部分共 7 个板块,其中语言输入部分的练习形式采用大学英语四、六级考试的 4 种题型,具有极强的针对性。具体单元设置如下表:

模块构思	板块设置	板块描述
导入	Viewing(视频导入)	通过与单元主题相关的精选视频导入本单元的主题,引发学生阅读兴趣

语言输入	Banked Cloze（集库式完形填空）	以集库式完形填空形式拓展学生的词汇量和语篇理解能力
	Long Passage（长篇速读）	以信息匹配形式提高学生的快速阅读（skimming and scanning）能力
	Short Passages（短篇细读）	通过多项选择题（multi-choice questions），全面提高学生的阅读理解能力，如掌握主旨（main idea）、找寻细节（details）、进行推断（inference）、词语释义（paraphrase）、判断态度（attitude）等能力
阅读技巧训练	Reading Skills（阅读技巧训练）	根据本单元阅读篇章特点，总结阅读技巧，并进行适度拓展练习，训练学生掌握这些阅读技巧
语言输出	Academic Words in Use（学术词汇训练）	精选本单元出现过的学术词汇，以集库式完形填空形式训练学生，让他们学会使用这些学术词汇，提高学生学术阅读能力，能用英语作为媒介学习学术内容
	Writing（写作训练）	通过写作训练复习本单元所学内容。训练题型有三种：一是大学英语四、六级考试作文题型；二是读后续写；三是单元内容小结

四、适用对象

本套教材适合我国普通高校一、二年级大学生使用，兼顾基础级别目标（第1、2册）和提高级别目标（第3、4册），并适度关注了学术词汇的学习。

五、教材使用建议

本套教材主要用于学生课下自学，可以与大学英语主干教材配套使用，也可以单独使用。

六、编写团队

本套教材总主编为上海海事大学李华东教授，第1—4册分别由温州商学院、内蒙古大学、浙江传媒学院和上海政法学院的教研团队编写。丛书编写方案由上海海事大学团队研发，主要成员包括朱莉雅、刘慧丹、陈园园、郝韵涵等。感谢清华大学出版社刘细珍老师在丛书策划、编写和成书过程中给予的大力支持。

本套教材系国家社会科学基金项目（17BYY103）部分成果。

由于编写时间紧，本套教材可能存在错漏和不妥之处，请教材使用者批评指正。

《新指南大学英语自主阅读》编写团队

2021年5月

Contents

Unit	Viewing	Banked Cloze	Long Passage
UNIT 1 Love — Page 1	Love Is an Open Door **About the video clip:** This video clip talks about the feeling of falling in love.	The Benefits of Marriage **NW:** 255 **GL:** 9.1 **AWL percentage:** 7.04% **Keywords:** benefit; couple; health	Students Don't Need You to Be a Prefect Teacher Right Now **NW:** 923 **GL:** 11.1 **AWL percentage:** 9.05% **Keywords:** universal love; care; education
UNIT 2 Growing Up — Page 21	Do Grades Matter? **About the video clip:** This video clip discusses the matter of grade in students' academic development by posing related questions and answering them with people's opinions and facts.	The Science Behind Why We Take Selfies **NW:** 359 **GL:** 11.8 **AWL percentage:** 6.39% **Keywords:** selfie; face; look	Personal Growth for a Truly Contented Life **NW:** 1,063 **GL:** 9.1 **AWL percentage:** 7.44% **Keywords:** personal growth; barriers; goals
UNIT 3 University Culture — Page 43	How to Balance College and Life **About the video clip:** This video clip suggests several ways for college students to better balance college and life.	Mission Statement of Suffolk University **NW:** 256 **GL:** 11.3 **AWL percentage:** 8.08% **Keywords:** university; mission statement; Suffolk University	What Are Universities For? **NW:** 984 **GL:** 12.4 **AWL percentage:** 6.71% **Keywords:** purpose; university; education
UNIT 4 Lifestyles I Like — Page 61	Maintaining a Healthy Balanced Lifestyle **About the video clip:** This video clip discusses 5 things we should think about for leading a healthy balanced lifestyle.	The Best Way to Find Balance in Your Life **NW:** 362 **GL:** 5.6 **AWL percentage:** 4.64% **Keywords:** balance; life; unstable	Should You Strive for Work/Life Balance? The History of the Personal & Professional Divide **NW:** 1,097 **GL:** 10.5 **AWL percentage:** 6.24% **Keywords:** life; balance; divide

Short Passages		Reading Skills	Academic Words in Use	Writing
Passage one Roses Lose Spell on Young Chinese Aged 30+ **NW:** 479 **GL:** 8.8 **AWL percentage:** 4.72% **Keywords:** Qixi; romance; stress	**Passage two** Why Everyone's Talking About the Cost of Weddings **NW:** 422 **GL:** 13.4 **AWL percentage:** 3.93% **Keywords:** wedding cost; burden; ceremony	Finding out Transitional Elements	traditional generation purchase priority survey reveal conduct perspective legal aware shift significantly	Do You Want to Celebrate Valentine's Day?
Passage one Sources of Stress and Anxiety in the Modern World **NW:** 635 **GL:** 10.5 **AWL percentage:** 7.78% **Keywords:** stress; anxiety; sources	**Passage two** Five Things You Must Know About College Degrees **NW:** 538 **GL:** 8.8 **AWL percentage:** 5.69% **Keywords:** college degrees; major; education	Patterns of Development	appraisal alternation self-conscious prescription perspective symptom efficient technical positive appealing specific ultimately	What Is Your Definition of Personal Growth?
Passage one College Life Changed Me: I Owe My New Personality to It **NW:** 432 **GL:** 11.4 **AWL percentage:** 6.7% **Keywords:** college life; personality; change	**Passage two** Why I Chose Yale **NW:** 373 **GL:** 11.2 **AWL percentage:** 1.59% **Keywords:** university; Yale; opportunity	Using Examples to Support Claims	aspect assignment available colleague energy focus goal grade lecture mental schedule stress	My View on the Postgraduate Craze
Passage one Work-Life Balance Is a Myth. Do This Instead **NW:** 485 **GL:** 8.8 **AWL percentage:** 4.09% **Keywords:** work; life; balance	**Passage two** Our Unhealthy Obsession with Entertainment **NW:** 367 **GL:** 9.3 **AWL percentage:** 5.15% **Keywords:** entertainment; addiction; American society	Drawing an Inference and a Conclusion	challenge despite editor individual issue majority philosopher physical previous rely survive job	Live a Healthy Life

Contents

Unit	Viewing	Banked Cloze	Long Passage
UNIT 5 **Emotion & Interaction** Page 81	Discipline Your Emotion **About the video clip:** This video clip discusses how to control your emotion.	First Impression NW: 249 GL: 9.3 AWL percentage: 6.43% Keywords: first impression; psychological factors; communication skill	Why You Shouldn't Always Look on the Bright Side NW: 822 GL: 10.0 AWL percentage: 9.23 % Keywords: interaction; optimism; understanding
UNIT 6 **Cooperation and Conflict** Page 99	What Is a Cooperative? **About the video clip:** This video clip discusses why cooperative is necessary, what is a cooperative and its benefits.	Why Team Work Matters for Children NW: 234 GL: 8.9 AWL percentage: 6.06% Keywords: teamwork; children; social skill	Anything Is Possible when China and the United States Choose to Cooperate NW: 1,029 GL: 10.2 AWL percentage: 5.76% Keywords: the United States; cooperation; China
UNIT 7 **Entrepreneurship** Page 117	How to Be an Entrepreneur? **About the video clip:** This video clip discusses how to become an entrepreneur.	Li Ziqi: A Blogger and Food Entrepreneur with One Foot in the Past and One Foot in the Future NW: 264 GL: 12.0 AWL percentage: 3.96% Keywords: sponsorship; launch; pursuit	A Work-Life Adventure NW: 994 GL: 9.7 AWL percentage: 5.1% Keywords: envision; digital nomad; inspiration
UNIT 8 **Career Development** Page 137	Apple CEO Tim Cook Talking About Career Planning **About the video clip:** This video clip discusses Apple CEO Tim Cook's thoughts on career plan.	Job Outlook Brightening for China Graduates NW: 296 GL: 12.0 AWL percentage: 8.25% Keywords: job outlook; ranking; employability	Should You Go to a Graduate School? NW: 797 GL: 12.3 AWL percentage: 6.29% Keywords: potential; reinvent; pioneer

Appendix: Video Script, Key and Sample Answers   153

Short Passages		Reading Skills	Academic Words in Use	Writing
Passage one People of All Ages **NW:** 308 **GL:** 9.7 **AWL percentage:** 5.19% **Keywords:** children; senior; social life	**Passage two** Children Can Still Detect Emotions Despite Face Masks **NW:** 332 **GL:** 12.2 **AWL percentage:** 5.53% **Keywords:** children; emotions; face masks	Sequencing Information	depress communicate location feature mental range expose expand response environment community benefit	Should Emotions Be Taught in Schools?
Passage one How to Say I'm Sorry (and Really Mean It) **NW:** 340 **GL:** 12.5 **AWL percentage:** 4.0% **Keywords:** apology; admission; contrition	**Passage two** The International Day of Friendship **NW:** 369 **GL:** 9.9 **AWL percentage:** 2.7% **Keywords:** international; friendship; celebration	Facts and Opinions	solution available privilege significant immense expect fulfill overwhelmingly tackling minimum capture instill	Competition or Cooperation, a Dilemma?
Passage one Meet the Entrepreneur Turning Your Footsteps into Energy **NW:** 333 **GL:** 9.1 **AWL percentage:** 4.51% **Keywords:** energy; radiate; innovation	**Passage two** The Man Who Sells Everything **NW:** 448 **GL:** 10.5 **AWL percentage:** 6.08% **Keywords:** entrepreneur; contemplate; breed	Reading Longer Passages Effectively	capture male launch industrial virtual fascinate affection annoy normal emission emphasize assign	My View on Entrepreneurship
Passage one What Should Every College Student Be Doing for Career Success? **NW:** 397 **GL:** 12.7 **AWL percentage:** 5.91% **Keywords:** career; internship; proactive	**Passage two** Lifelong Learning Is Becoming an Economic Imperative **NW:** 292 **GL:** 12.4 **AWL percentage:** 8.01% **Keywords:** lifelong learning; imperative; occupations	Being an Active Reader	like-minded engine cognitive origin educational fulfilment recycle switch trigger fierce acquire feature	On College Students' Career Planning

Viewing

Love Is an Open Door

About the video clip

This video clip talks about the feeling of falling in love.

Understanding the video clip

Please watch the video clip and fill in the blanks in the table below.

Anna	Hans
She and Elsa were close when they were young, but one day Elsa _____.	He was just _____ the same thing, because he had been _____ his whole life.
She felt her life was _____ doors, then suddenly _____ Hans.	He said they would _____ to the _____ of the past.
With Hans she found _____, she saw _____.	He felt love can be so _____ with her.
Anna thought their _____ synchronization can have but one _____	At last, he asked _____.
Finally, Anna say something even _____, yes.	

Further thoughts

Anna and Hans fell in love at the first sight. Could you list the advantages and disadvantages of "fall in love at the first sight"?

Advantages	Disadvantages
1. full of enthusiasm	1. not lasting for a long time
2. arousing the inside power instantly	2. always hurtful
...	...

Banked Cloze

Below is a passage with ten blanks. You are required to select one word for each blank from the list of choices given in a word bank following the passage. Read the passage carefully before making your choices. Each choice in the blank is identified by a letter. Please write the corresponding letter for each item in the blanks. You may not use any of the words in the bank more than once.

The Benefits of Marriage[1]

NW: 255 **GL:** 9.1 **AWL percentage:** 7.04% **Keywords:** benefit; couple; health

Being sociable looks like a good way to add years to your life. Relationships with family, friends, neighbors, even 1._____, will all do the trick, but the biggest longevity boost seems to come from marriage or a(n) 2._____ relationship. The effect was first noted in 1858 by William Farr, who wrote that widows and widowers were at a much 3._____ risk of dying than their married 4._____. Studies since then suggest that marriage could add as much as seven years to a man's life and two to a woman's. The effect holds for all causes of death, whether illness, accident or self-harm.

Even if the odds are stacked against you, marriage can more than compensate. Linda Waite of the University of Chicago has found that a married old man with heart disease can

---

1 From CNBlogs website.

5._____ to live nearly four years longer than an unmarried man with a healthy heart. 6._____, a married man who 7._____ more than a pack a day is likely to live as long as a divorced man who doesn't smoke. There is a flip side, however, as partners are more likely to become ill or die in the couple of years following their 8._____'s death, and caring for a spouse with mental disorder can leave you with some of the same severe problems. Even so, the odds favor 9._____. In a 30-year study of more than 10,000 people, Nicholas Christakis of Harvard Medical School 10._____ how all kinds of social networks have similar effects.

A) spouse	B) divorce	C) expect
D) describes	E) smokes	F) higher
G) families	H) lower	I) equivalent
J) pets	K) likewise	L) same
M) However	N) marriage	O) peers

Long Passage

You are going to read a passage with ten statements attached to it. Each statement contains information given in one of the paragraphs. Identify the paragraph from which the information is derived. You may choose a paragraph more than once. Each paragraph is marked with a letter. Please answer the questions by writing the corresponding letter after the statements.

Students Don't Need You to Be a Perfect Teacher Right Now[2]

NW: 923   GL: 11.1   AWL percentage: 9.05%   Keywords: universal love; care; education

A   In early March my university administration informed me that I had a week to transition my University of Virginia course Books Behind Bars online. This is a class I've been teaching for the past decade, where UVA students meet regularly with incarcerated youth at Bon Air Juvenile Correctional Center[3] in Richmond[4], Virginia to explore questions of meaning, value, and social justice through conversations about the Russian literature.

---

2 From Newsweek website.
3 Juvenile Correctional Center: 少年管教中心
4 Richmond: 里士满,美国弗吉尼亚州首府

B   At first I thought I'd be able to salvage the core of my class—the powerful interactions between the university and correctional center students—through virtual Zoom[5] or telephone meetings. But then COVID struck in the correctional center, eventually infecting one-eighth of the youth population there. Facility-wide medical lockdowns followed, making any communication between the two groups impossible. My class, it seemed, was dead in the water.

C   The semester is now over, and I was never able to bring back the face-to-face meetings between UVA and Bon Air students. Nor was there any hope of resurrecting the student relationships because of the facility's "no-contact" policy preventing outside volunteers from maintaining contact with correctional center residents after a program ends. This is not what I'd envisioned for the tenth-anniversary interaction of my class.

D   But if I had dwelled on what was gone, I would have lost my ability to harness what was still present. In a time of crises such as we're in now, we are all students again in a sense, trying to rebuild the broken ship of our lives while sailing on it toward an unknown destination. Full-time working parents are taking on a second full-time jobs as homeschool teachers for which most have no training.

E   Front-line healthcare workers confront COVID's catastrophic toll, while sometimes forced to make heart-wrenching decisions about who gets life-saving treatments and who doesn't. Religious institutions, government agencies, nonprofits, corporations, and private individuals are doing what they can to alleviate human suffering amid fear and uncertainty and without any rule books to guide them.

F   None of us are experts in navigating these unprecedented waters. We're a community of learners facing the unknown together. So how can teachers best support students in this process? Or parents their children, healthcare workers their patients, all of us one another? The answers to these questions are more similar than we might think. Whether you're a tenth-grade biology teacher or a parent homeschooling your four-year-old, the content of your teaching matters far less in this moment than the attitudes and values you're modeling and life skills you're helping the students develop for themselves.

G   Shortly after my class as I knew it had been gutted, I had to face the realization that it was no longer about what I thought it was about. It became a course now on how human beings caught in extraordinarily difficult circumstances can still practice empathy, summon imagination, and maintain hope.

H   John Dewey, educational philosopher and one of the foremost proponents of

---

5 Zoom: 一款多人手机云视频会议软件

experiential education, said that "all genuine learning comes through experience but not all experiences are genuinely or equally educative." As the pandemic wreaks havoc on our world, we all have been thrust into one of the most challenging experiential learning classes of our lifetimes.

I   Whether this crisis becomes an opportunity for personal growth—"educative", to use Dewey's word—or simply a tragic memory years from now will depend on the meaning we make out of it and the lessons we take from it.

J   My students have taken inspiration from the examples of people creating human connection in the midst of fear and isolation. Many students developed videos of themselves sharing personal thoughts about life and literature, imagining the correctional center residents were still sitting right next to them. Other students wrote heartfelt letters to the residents, correspondents they know they will never see again. Still others honored the memory of the relationships they'd built through social action projects advocating for incarcerated youth.

K   Students in Books Behind Bars knew all along that their relationships with the correctional center residents would end at some point. But none of us could have predicted just how abruptly and unexpectedly that end would come. Not having had the chance to say goodbye, my UVA students feel sad and incomplete. They continue to worry about the residents and wonder if they'll be OK.

L   My task as a teacher through this rupture was not to lecture, but to listen to and support students in their process of making meaning out of what seems to them a meaningless, terrifying moment. I've long viewed my role as a college teacher less as a purveyor of expert knowledge than as a facilitator of student learning and personal growth. I learned from my best instructors over the years that good teachers start with the student, not the subject. Never has this mindset been more essential.

M   Some of my most influential teachers never worked in any kind of formal classroom. They were the people I encountered growing up who were concerned with my well-being, listened to me, encouraged me to take risks, and taught me valuable life lessons not by words but by example.

N   Students don't need me to be a perfect teacher right now. They need me to be honest and human, to let them know that I, too, have never been here before and that we'll figure this out together. Students, like the rest of us, have been traumatized. They wonder what this all means, and when it will end. They have connectivity issues. Some are cooped up at home in unhealthy relationships with parents or caring for ailing relatives. Others are scrambling to find work just to stay afloat. High-school and college seniors have been robbed of the rite of passage known as graduation.

0   Academic learning isn't their top priority right now. Nor should it be.

1. Students were undergoing some unexpected problems right now.
2. It's hard for the doctors to make a decision on who should be saved first.
3. Some young people were infected with COVID, so the whole center was shut down.
4. Experience is the real root of the authentic study.
5. Sometimes there is no such day for us to say goodbye to each other.
6. The writer's course now can help people rouse hope.
7. To "me", the most important thing right now was to guide the students to find the value of life.
8. Students used their ways to encourage each other.
9. The significance and lessons of the crisis would help us see it clearly.
10. Most of the time the valuable knowledge is not acquired in the classroom.

Short Passages

There are two passages in this module. Each passage is followed by some questions or unfinished statements. For each of them there are four choices marked A, B, C, and D. You should decide on the best choice and mark the corresponding letter.

Passage one

Roses Lose Spell on Young Chinese Aged 30+[6]

NW: 479 **GL:** 8.8 **AWL percentage:** 4.72% **Keywords:** Qixi; romance; stress

Today the Chinese celebrate their traditional Valentine's Day[7] known as Qixi[8]. Like in the West, young Chinese express their love through roses.

Data shows that people under the age of 30 are the biggest buyers of roses and that those over 30 are not so keen on the flowers. Is that because love fades as one gets older, or is there a deeper reason behind it?

Love is in the air as the Chinese Valentine's Day arrives. On the streets of Beijing, and

---

6 From CCTV ENGLISH website.
7 Valentine's Day: 又被称为 St. Valentine's Day，即圣瓦伦丁节，情人节。
8 Qixi: 农历七月初七，有祈福许愿、坐看牵牛织女星、祈祷姻缘等传统习俗，又被称为"中国情人节"。

in shopping centers, flower shops are seeing their business bloom. Roses are love birds' top pick when it comes to gifts.

Analysts say China's post-90s generation is the most active in preparing for roses.

"Over 50 percent of the people that conduct searches on Taobao and Tmall to buy roses are under the age of 24. And over 90 percent are people aged below 30. They are mainly male, white collars, and students," said Yang Qin, chief analyst, CBNData[9].

Data also shows that people between the ages of 35 and 40 have the lowest interest in roses. They are even less enthusiastic than those in their 40s.

Yang says part of the reason for that is that romance fades after marriage. "From a rather pessimistic perspective, most people above the age of 30 have gotten married, and they express their love less and less frequently," he said.

Another reason is that older couples are more stable financially and have additional choices besides just flowers. "Our customers who are a bit older usually like to purchase products that improve the quality of life, such as home fragrances, and jewellery. People in their 30s and 40s have more practical needs, such as socialization purposes," said Huang Lijiang, sales specialist, The Beast[10].

For some, the price tag for romance is simply too unrealistic. "The idea of buying roses didn't even cross my mind. We are in the age bracket of 30 to 40, our career is only half-way to the top, we are paying mortgages for our apartments in Beijing. It's a period with the heaviest financial pressure," said Feng Anan, legal officer.

Anan said that because Beijing's property prices are so high, the top priority is to pay off their bank loans.

"We used to go to the concerts, or buy luxury goods, but now we don't prepare gifts for each other. The first thought we have each month after getting paid, is how we can pay off our mortgage quicker. That's the reality," she said.

Heavy financial pressure is one of the main contributors to China's high divorce rate among the post-80s generation. But Anan entered her marriage fully aware of the harsh reality and said that as long as they love and support each other, every day is Valentine's Day.

9　CBNData: 第一财经商业数据中心
10　The Beast: 野兽派，2011年建立的家居品牌，产品包括花艺、香氛、家纺、家具等。

1. **Who is the least potential customer to buy roses at Qixi according to the passage?**

   A. A college student.

   B. A sales manager below 30.

   C. A teacher at his 30s.

   D. A CEO at his 40s.

2. **What can we infer from the CBNData?**

   A. Over 50% of the people looking for roses online are under the age of 20.

   B. People looking for roses online are only male, white collars and students.

   C. People between the ages of 35 and 40 don't have enough interest in roses.

   D. Women customers are becoming more and more.

3. **People between 35 and 40 didn't want to buy roses because _____.**

   A. they expressed their love less and less frequently

   B. the romance between the couples gradually faded after marriage

   C. they had other choices besides roses

   D. all of the above

4. **Feng Anan's example is used to express that _____.**

   A. the high price of the house limits the desire to buy roses

   B. for some people, the price tag for romance is simply too unrealistic

   C. the stress of life destroys the love between husband and wife

   D. the mid-aged couples are indifferent to such a romantic day

5. **Which reason can directly lead to the rising divorce rate according to the passage?**

   A. The working pressure.

   B. The financial pressure.

   C. The psychological pressure.

   D. The parenting burden.

Passage two

Why Everyone's Talking About the Cost of Weddings[11]

NW: 422   **GL:** 13.4   **AWL percentage:** 3.93%   **Keywords:** wedding cost; burden; ceremony

Weddings are becoming a burden for millennials who are struggling with the expense of increasingly costly celebrations.

One in seven guests will <u>fork out</u> more than £400 to attend a wedding this summer, and some will pay up to £1,000 to join in the celebrations, says *The Times*[12].

One in three millennials get themselves in debt in an effort to attend friends' weddings, while one in four admitted they had missed rent payments or failed to cover their bills to cover the costs, according to a survey of renters by Spareroom.co.uk.

With a 2017 report from Office for National Statistics finding that the average UK renter was paying 27% of their gross salary to their landlord in 2016—and Londoners paying 49%—it's no surprise that Generation Rent is starting to dodge expensive weddings.

A third of those questioned by SpareRoom.co.uk admitted turning down wedding invitations, and 20% said they had fallen out with friends over the cost of attending. An American Express[13] study earlier this year found that wedding guests spend an average of £391. That's nearly a third more than last year, according to *The Evening Standard*.

Why are weddings so expensive for guests?

The Amex wedding study breaks down the £391 average wedding costs for guests in order of expense: hotel (£72), outfit(£68), gift(£66), hen/stag(£58), travel(£57), drinks(£45), hair and beauty(£25)

The cost is partly down to the growing numbers of couples getting hitched overseas, which can reduce their costs but shifts the burden on to their guests.

A 2018 report by tourism company Kuoni revealed that the average spend on a foreign wedding destination is £7,500, compared to more than £27,000 in the UK. But while tying the knot[14] in your favorite holiday destination might not break the bank of

---

11 From THE WEEK website.
12 *The Times*: 一般称《泰晤士报》，是英国的一张综合性全国发行的日报，对全球的政治、经济、文化产生巨大影响。
13 American Express: 美国运通公司
14 try the knot: 结为连理

the happy couple, it increases the costs of travel for invitees. A study by Hotels.com found that the cost of attending a wedding overseas was significantly more than attending one in the UK. Guests at overseas weddings had to fork out an average £2,050 to cover the extra flights, hotels, insurance and luggage, reports *The Independent*[15].

Are wedding couples paying more too?

The average cost of a wedding in the UK this year is £31,974, 54% higher than £20,799 in 2014—and the main reason for the price hike is social media pressure according to Hitched's National Wedding Survey 2019.

1. Which verb can be replaced the underlined phrase "fork out" in Para. 2?

A. Spend.

B. Use.

C. Have.

D. Waste.

2. Why does getting married overseas shift the burden onto guests?

A. Because guests may not like the wedding destination chosen by the couple.

B. Because the popular holiday destination will spent all the money of the couple.

C. Because the overseas wedding is too expensive to afford for the couple.

D. Because it increases the cost of travel for guests.

3. Which one is TRUE according to the passage?

A. The newly-married couple will have more friends because of the wedding.

B. Every wedding invitation was accepted by the guests.

C. Generation Rent avoids going to weddings due to their high spending on rent.

D. The guests love to go to the wedding no matter how expensive it will be.

4. What is the main reason for the couple spending more on the wedding?

A. The pressure from social media.

B. They want to have an overseas wedding.

---

15 *The Independent*: 即《独立报》，是英国最具影响力的全国性报纸之一。

C. They prepare a lot of luxurious gifts for the guests.

D. They love to have a great celebration.

5. **According to the passage, which one is the best description about the wedding?**

A. Many young couples want to have a romantic overseas wedding.

B. The young generation is increasingly rejecting the wedding invitation.

C. Wedding cost has become a burden between friends.

D. In order to attend the wedding, the government should reduce the rent charge.

Reading Skills

Finding out Transitional Elements

Transitional elements or transitional signals are useful words or phrases for helping the reader grasp the connections in a paragraph. These connecting words or phrases permit easy passage from one sentence or idea to the next. Words like "first", "next", "for example" are like road signs, helping to point the way, to keep the direction clear. They tie ideas together in a paragraph.

There are a number of ways transitions relate sentences or ideas. They may show that something is added, repeated, or intensified; they may compare or contrast two things; they may show time order in which actions take place; they may show a cause and effect relationship. The following list groups the commonly used transitions according to their function.

1. To add ideas together:

and, also, besides, furthermore, in addition, moreover, too, first, second, finally

2. To show emphasis and clarity:

above all, after all, in fact, particularly, that is

3. To show similarity:

like, likewise, in the same manner, in the same way, similarly

4. To show contrast:

although, but, however, in comparison, in contrast, in spite of, on the contrary, on the other hand, unlike, whereas, while, yet

5. To express cause and effect relationship:

as, because, due to, for, for this reason, now that, since, owing to, as a result, accordingly, consequently, therefore, thus

6. To point out examples:

for example, for instance, to illustrate

7. To draw a conclusion, an inference, or a summary:

in a word, in conclusion, in brief, in short, in summary, to conclude, to summarize, to sum up, therefore

8. To indicate time:

at times, after, afterward, from then on, immediately, later, meanwhile, next, now, then, until, while

Exercises

Please read the above reading skill of finding out transitional elements and use the guidelines to find the different types of the transitional elements in Short Passage One entitled "Roses Lose Spell on Young Chinese Aged 30+".

Transitional elements are :

_____

_____

THINK

Academic Words in Use

Fill in the blanks in the following sentences with the appropriate words provided in the box below. Change the form of the words if necessary.

traditional	generation	purchase	priority	survey	reveal
conduct	perspective	legal	aware	shift	significantly

1. It is _____ for the bridegroom to make a speech.
2. In the intense atmosphere, the director _____ the conversation to a more comfortable subject.
3. Many students go to university to acquire a broader _____ of life.
4. People use money to _____ goods and services.
5. Most smokers are perfectly _____ of the dangers of smoking.
6. A recent _____ was conducted by the University of Manchester into children's attitudes towards violence on television.
7. Methods used by young teachers differ _____ from those used by older ones.
8. The newspaper story _____ a cover-up of huge proportions.
9. If medical supplies are short, children will be given _____.
10. China has developed a(n) _____ system to promote technology transfer.
11. We are the fourth _____ of Carters to live in this house.
12. The company _____ a research to find out local reaction to the leisure center.

Writing

For this part, you are allowed 30 minutes to read the following paragraphs and continue writing to make it a well-structured article. You should write at least 120 words but no more than 180 words.

Do You Want to Celebrate Valentine's Day?

Valentine's day is approaching and people in many parts of the world are getting ready to lighten their wallets for their loved ones. Eating out, buying presents, chocolates or flowers for their significant others have become a tradition on this particular day. It is definitely the day of love in the world and has also spread its roots to every corner of the earth.

Originally, Valentine's day was celebrated in the West to honor Saint Valentine from Rome, who was imprisoned and executed for performing illegal weddings for persecuted Christians.

Unit 2 Growing Up

Viewing

Do Grades Matter?

About the video clip

This video clip discusses the matter of grade in students' academic development by posing related questions and answering them with people's opinions and facts.

Understanding the video clip

Watch the video clip and fill in the blanks in the table below.

Questions	Opinions and facts
1. Do good grades actually matter?	Most of a person's young life _____ around school, waking up every day at the crack of _____, carrying an ungodly amount of books, and working towards good grades that will _____ help them get into a good college and a good job. Students are constantly asking, "Do good grades actually matter?" "Is my life _____ by the grades I get in school?"
2. What are the results of NPR poll?	A 2013 NPR poll found that nearly _____ of parents believed their high schooler feels high levels of school related stress. Some _____ of grade anxiety might be increased heart rate, _____, and decreased appetite. Being a kid should be fun, right?

3. Can tests be able to account for important areas, like critical thinking?	One school of thought is that these tests are unable to _____ for important areas, like critical thinking, _____, and imagination. Will memorizing vocabulary _____ you to a better future? According to a survey by the National Association of Colleges and Employers, 78.3% of employers claim to _____ future employees by GPA. However, 63.5% of employers only use a 3.0 as a GPA cutoff for employment. So, pushing yourself to be above average may not mean much in the long run.
4. What is people's another worry?	There's also the worry that schools are _____ their curriculums around the test. This is believed to be a result of incentive systems put in place by the Department of Education that _____ schools with higher test scores. A _____ by New York governor Andrew Cuomo would have 50% of a teacher's _____ correlate to the result of their student's scores.
5. What is real education?	Education should be _____ and expressive, _____ to student's needs and wants, not based around a system of points. What if you just want to paint some stuff or write some stuff?
6. So, do grades matter?	Yes and no. If you're looking to _____ a path of higher education, then yeah, they do matter. But don't stress about grades. Everyone's _____ is different, and chances are you won't even remember your SAT score in five years. Whatever you focus on, just try to the best of your ability, whatever that may be. The _____ of effort you put into something will always say more than a letter on a report card.

Further thoughts

Grade has always been the focus of concern in people's academic development. Should grade be the main criterion for judging a person's qualification? List the possible reasons for both sides of opinions in the table below.

Yes	No
1. Grade can be the most effective way for selecting talents.	1. Grade does not measure a person's intelligence, creativity and critical thinking.
2. Grade can indicate the effort people put into the thing in concern.	2. Grade is just one dimension of a whole person.
…	…

Banked Cloze

Below is a passage with ten blanks. You are required to select one word for each blank from the list of choices given in a word bank following the passage. Read the passage carefully before making your choices. Each choice in the blank is identified by a letter. Please write the corresponding letter for each item in the blanks. You may not use any of the words in the bank more than once.

The Science Behind Why We Take Selfies[1]

NW: 359　**GL:** 11.8　**AWL percentage:** 6.39%　**Keywords:** selfie; face; look

The selfie has arguably become the greatest photographic trend of our time. "Why are we so interested in taking and sharing selfies and how does observing an image of yourself differ from 1._____ a picture of someone else?" asked University College London neuroscientist James Kilner.

In everyday social situations we spend a lot of our time looking at and interpreting other people's faces and facial expressions. Indeed, reading and responding correctly to other people's facial expressions is 2._____ for successful social interactions.

Through our lifetimes we become experts at recognizing and interpreting other people's faces and facial expressions. In contrast, we have very little experience of looking at

---

1　From BBC website.

our own faces.

Our 3._____ of our own facial expression comes from our sense of feeling our faces move. This lack of 4._____ knowledge about our own faces means we have a very inaccurate representation of what our own faces look like at any given time. For example, it has been 5._____ that when people are shown an image of themselves and asked to match it they are unable to 6._____ produce the same facial expression without being able to see themselves.

This lack of knowledge about what we look like has a(n) 7._____ effect on what we think we look like. When people are asked to pick a photograph which they think looks most like them—from a series of photographs in which an actual photograph has been digitally 8._____ to produce more attractive and less attractive versions—people are very bad at selecting the original photograph.

Given that we have a poor representation of what we look like, this is perhaps unsurprising. What is surprising is that people systematically choose images that have been digitally altered to make the person appear more attractive.

In other words, we have an image of ourselves that 9._____ to be younger and more attractive than we actually are.

This might in part explain our 10._____ with selfies. For the first time we are able to take and retake pictures of ourselves until we can produce an image that come closer to matching our perception of what we think we look like.

A) essential	B) demonstrated	C) perception
D) accurately	E) profound	F) taking
G) relationship	H) requires	I) visual
J) observing	K) tends	L) mainly
M) obsession	N) basic	O) altered

Long Passage

You are going to read a passage with ten statements attached to it. Each statement contains information given in one of the paragraphs. Identify the paragraph from which the information is derived. You may choose a paragraph more than once. Each paragraph is marked with a letter. Please answer the questions by writing the corresponding letter after the statements.

Personal Growth for a Truly Contented Life[2]

NW: 1,063 **GL:** 9.1 **AWL percentage:** 7.44% **Keywords:** personal growth; barriers; goals

A   Personal growth is a consistent approach to improve the level of self-knowledge and to ensure growth in every aspect of life, such as mental, physical and spiritual, for the maximization of inherent potential to lead a truly contented life. Personal growth is an ongoing process. There is no such thing like limits or saturation point associated with personal growth. No matter at what stages of life you are, you can always find something to learn and grow as a person. Personal growth makes a person better today than yesterday. It is your personal growth, which is going to remain with you forever. It becomes the intrinsic part of your personality. Your personal growth defines your own individuality—the core of your unique personality.

---

2 From kavikishor website.

B   By the very personal growth definition, the area of personal growth is mental, physical and spiritual. There are great interrelations among each area of personal growth. A healthy physic is essential for proper development of mind, and the growth in mental and physical areas cannot be beneficial for humanity in general without the good character, which are built by spirituality.

C   Personal growth and development is a life-long process, and everyone has the capacity to learn and grow throughout the life. Although personal growth is essential for everyone to have a contented life, keeping focus on one area over the others does not fulfill the requirement of what we mean by personal growth. Maintaining a balance and giving attention to each area is very much essential to realize the personal growth goal in life.

D   Self-knowledge is the foundation for personal growth and spiritual understanding. It is the self-knowledge that defines the path for your personal growth. The simple rule is that, "to raise the height of your personal growth, you must increase the level of your self-knowledge."

E   The self-knowledge helps you to understand your real self, your strength as well as your weaknesses. In other words, self-knowledge is the stepping stone to walk down to the personal growth path. Once you understand your real self, you can chart-out the road-map for your personal growth.

F   According to the law of nature, all living things, including we all human being, are either growing or dying. Growth is the sign of life. Whether you embrace personal growth or not, changes are bound to happen in yourself and around you with each passing fraction of time. Changing is the only thing which remains constant in life. It is an automatic process. It does not require your permission to happen. Everything in this world is constantly changing. However, experiencing changes in yourself and in the world around you are not an indication of growth.

G   Most people do not deal with changes in a positive way to learn and grow in life and because of that they become stagnant due to their consistent desire of living in their comfort zone[3]. The changes bring paralyzing fear for them about what life ahead. The desire to live within the comfort zone is the prime reason to halt personal growth in life. It makes the person feel uncomfortable to do things in a different way and have varied experiences in life, which are crucial for personal growth. Unless a person chooses to deal with changes confidently, personal growth is not possible for them. Personal growth is a choice. You have to make a conscious choice to move past your fear of unknown in

---

3 comfort zone: 舒适区

order to make personal growth.

H Just wishing to pace the growth of life is not enough. You have to work hard for making progress in life, and at the same time you have to overcome the hurdles on the way to personal growth and development. To overcome the barriers to personal growth and development, you need to identify what kind of obstacles is holding you back from achieving your desired goal in life. There are commonly two kinds of barriers to personal growth and development.

I The biggest barrier to personal growth and development is the lack of self-esteem[4]. Most of the people used to compare themselves with other people who are successful in life and develop a mindset[5] that they are not worthy enough to achieve anything extraordinary in life. Due to low self-worth, they do not dare to follow their desired goal. However, the fact of matter is that everyone has their unique capability, and the ultimate potential of everyone is the same. So, it is waste of time to engage in comparing yourself with others and underestimate yourself in any way. Increase the level of self-esteem and follow your desired goal in life. You are destined to enjoy the beauty of life provided you keep you head high and follow your goals in life.

J Procrastination is another barrier to personal growth and development. You will gain very little in life if you keep delaying things. The best moment to act on the personal growth and development is now. No matter how great your goals are and what capacity you have, if you keep on procrastinating it is guaranteed that you will remain underachiever in life. So, stop procrastination and aim for personal growth and development in every situation.

K The goal of personal growth and development is very much personal for everyone. As the meaning of personal growth varies from person to person at any given time, so are their respective goals. Therefore, it is not wise to compare yourself with others because everyone has the different personal growth goals best suited to their requirement.

L Personal growth is about being your better self, not a perfect one. The best part of personal growth is that you can go for it anytime no matter at what stages of life you are. There is always an opportunity available to make improvement and make your life a little bit better than it is supposed to be.

M Hence, you should always aim to achieve some personal growth goals in every aspect of life to develop as a mentally, physically and spiritually strong individual. The

---

4 self-esteem: 自尊，一个沿自西方的学术性概念，指的是个体对自我能力和自我价值的一种评价性情感体验。
5 mindset: 思维模式，影响决策和行为的一套态度、思想和情感。

energy and time invested in achieving personal growth goal will not only make you confident enough to face problems of life head-on but also fill your life with success and happiness. So, follow your goals for personal growth in every situation to have a truly contented life.

1. Personal growth is based on the understanding of oneself in every aspect. ☐
2. Personal growth refers to a way to make a person better by improving the level of self-knowledge and ensuring growth in every aspect of life, so that the person can enjoy a real happy life. ☐
3. Though changes are inevitable in a human life, growth is not a process of merely going through changes. ☐
4. Personal growth is a proactive choice to face the unknown and challenge the inner tendency of staying in a familiar environment. ☐
5. Personal growth is about making improvement by overcoming all kinds of barriers. ☐
6. People with less confidence will encounter more challenges on their way of personal growth. ☐
7. Personal growth could be influenced by the bad habit of postponing things in one's life. ☐
8. The goal of personal growth varies from person to person. ☐
9. Personal growth can happen at any time either making a better person or a better life for one. ☐
10. Achieving personal growth goal will offer one with a successful and happy life. ☐

Short Passages

There are two passages in this module. Each passage is followed by some questions or unfinished statements. For each of them there are four choices marked A, B, C, and D. You should decide on the best choice and mark the corresponding letter.

Passage one

Sources of Stress and Anxiety in the Modern World[6]

NW: 635 **GL:** 10.5 **AWL percentage:** 7.78% **Keywords:** stress; anxiety; sources

Humans have been a high-stress bunch for much of our history, but our collective mental health has taken an especially significant hit over the past few months. In April, the UK Office for National Statistics found that 84.2 percent of Britons were worried about COVID-19 and its effects on their lives, whilst a staggering 46.9 percent said they had "high levels of anxiety."

But the ongoing global pandemic isn't the only reason people have found it hard to smile lately. And although managing stress and anxiety isn't as simple as "shifting your

---

6 From Reader's digest website.

perspective" or "thinking positive" (despite the deluge of inspiring Instagram[7] memes[8] to the contrary), there are things you can do to feel better.

Let's take a closer look at what can trigger those tough feelings, and what can help you cope with them.

What causes stress and anxiety?

First, stress and anxiety are different. Feelings of stress generally arise in response to a specific situation or circumstance. As the National Health Service (NHS) explains, anxiety disorders are chronic conditions whose origins can be more complex. However, both stress and anxiety are often triggered by concerns around:

Health: Aside from the pandemic itself, pre-existing conditions like high blood pressure and cancer can cause a great deal of worry. **Money:** Each month the bills keep coming, and they never seem to get any smaller. **Precarious employment:** The "gig economy[9]" and "flexi-work[10]" have turned out to be much less appealing than promised. **Social/political conflict:** If you haven't read the papers or seen the news on TV, there's quite a lot of it at the moment. **Relationship issues:** Nobody knows how to push our buttons better than our partners, children, family members, and friends.

Now, let's see how you can help alleviate the feelings these issues produce.

How do people reduce stress and anxiety?

People have developed a wide range of coping strategies for dealing with stress and anxiety over the years. But as UK mental health charity Mind put it, self-care for anxiety is extra challenging right now, and it's normal if your old methods seem out of reach right now. That being said, another option might be more feasible:

Prescription medication: Doctors can prescribe antidepressants and similar drugs if needed. **Meditation and breathing exercises:** Spending some time each day in silence helps many people find their center. **Therapy:** Talking to a licensed therapist or joining a group can offer an outlet for difficult feelings. **Exercise:** Going for a run or lifting weights can release brain chemicals that boost your mood. **Natural supplements:** Many people have turned to plant-based remedies as an alternative to pharmaceuticals. It's common for people to try multiple methods at once, depending on their needs and preferences.

---

7 Instagram: 照片墙，一款运行在移动端上的社交应用平台
8 meme: 模因，也称为米姆、弥、弥因、弥母、迷因、文化基因等，是文化信息传承时的单位。模因，目前比较公认的定义是"一个想法、行为或风格从一个人到另一个人的文化传播过程"。
9 gig economy: 零工经济是指由工作量不多的自由职业者构成的经济领域，利用互联网和移动技术快速匹配供需方，主要包括群体工作和经应用程序接洽的按需工作两种形式。
10 flexi-work: 灵活工作，flexi 是 flexible 的缩写。

What method of reducing stress and anxiety is best for you?

If you've lived with stress and anxiety before—and if you're reading this article, we assume you have—you already know there's no "one size fits all" solution for getting your internal narrator to calm down a bit. Instead, the best option is to take a careful appraisal of your personality and set an intentional path forward.

For example: If you're a person who can't sit still no matter how hard you try, going for runs might be more helpful than trying to meditate for a half hour each morning. And if you prefer to avoid putting lab-made chemicals in your body, you might opt for an organic supplement like CBD (provided it's from a reputable company).

The most important thing to remember is to stay consistent. It would be wonderful if any of these solutions instantly erased your stress and anxiety, but in all likelihood this is a long game. However, if you stick with your program (whilst still staying responsive to any new needs that pop up), you can come out on top.

1. **The example of "COVID-19 related anxiety" is used to _____.**
   A. indicate that the stress people feel presently is from the pandemic
   B. be the example of common phenomena of people feeling anxiety
   C. tell the reader health-related issues are the main source of anxiety
   D. imply that people nowadays are feeling anxiety with no good reason

2. **Which of the following statements is INCORRECT according to the passage?**
   A. Different things could be the combined reasons for causing stress and anxiety.
   B. There are all kinds of ways to deal with stress and anxiety.
   C. There is no such thing as a magical method to reduce stress instantly.
   D. If we want to reduce stress and anxiety we should try out all the methods mentioned.

3. **What does the underlined phrase out of reach (Line 3, Para. 7) mean?**
   A. Unaccessible.
   B. Useless.
   C. Reachable.
   D. Applicable.

4. **What can we infer from the last paragraph?**

A. One of the solutions mentioned above is bound to reduce your stress.

B. Stress and anxiety only exist for a while in your life time.

C. We should get ready to deal with stress for a long time and explore the best way to reduce it.

D. If there is a new kind of stress we should always stick to our stress-reducing solution.

5. **From the passage, we can conclude that _____.**

A. stress and anxiety are common for all people and we should have a clear understanding of them

B. different people will have the same kind of ways to deal with various kind of stress

C. stress and anxiety are just emotional or psychological phenomena

D. stress and anxiety only exist within certain group of people

Passage two

Five Things You Must Know About College Degrees[11]

NW: 538   **GL:** 8.8   **AWL percentage:** 5.69%   **Keywords:** college degrees; major; education

Are you getting ready to begin college, head back to school after a few years off, or maybe just exploring your options? If so, it's important to know a few of the basic facts about modern day degrees. Things have changed a lot in the past few years. Here's a quick overview of five key facts that will serve you well as you aim for an education credential.

Online study can save you big bucks

In the modern technical society, it's becoming easier to attend school online. If you choose a school's online program, it's possible to save as much as 50 percent over in-person options. So, unless you have some special reason for attending in person, check out all your choices. Be aware that institutions that offer telecommuting and online study sometimes have a more limited range of courses and majors for those e-degree programs. Spend time seeing if your desired subjects are part of the e-curriculum wherever you decide to apply.

Arrange financing first

Getting your degree and paying for it are two completely different challenges. That's why it's essential to get financing arranged before you choose your college or pick your major. If you don't have the money situation taken care of, schools simply won't let you begin the coursework. The good news is that you can take out a student loan from a private lender and get the entire payment issue resolved quickly. Plus, you can arrange to cover major and minor expenses, including tuition, campus activity fees, board, room/dorm rent, textbook purchases, and more. Using private student loans is a simple, fast, and smart way to get from square one to the classroom and begin earning your diploma.

Do career research before choosing a major

It's important to choose a major that has realistic job prospects for graduates. You might love art history or linguistic philosophy, but unless you intend to restrict your career to teaching, check out some majors that are more practical, like accounting, IT, advertising, engineering, and more. Ask the school reps what their most popular majors are, what job placement rates are, and whether they offer internships for seniors in their fields of study.

---

11 From Reader's digest website.

Spend time on application essays

When you fill out applications for the schools that interest you, don't just rush through the paperwork. Some of it is standard, fill-in-the-blank information. But most apps usually contain at least one essay-type question. You'll need to be careful when filling out these kinds of items. Admissions offices tend to focus on your essay, scores on standardized tests, grades, and job history. Don't worry if you have scant work experience or if it's been several years since you attended high school. But take at least one hour per 300 words on each essay. Most applications ask you to write at least 1,200 words, so expect to spend a full four hours planning, outlining, composing, and editing.

It's possible to work while earning a degree

Be careful about working and attending school at the same time. Try to keep job hours to part-time or less. If you're attending classes on a part-time basis, then it's easier to work more than part-time.

1. According to Paragraph 2, people should consider all the things EXCEPT _____ when it comes to attending online school.

    A. all kinds of expenses on campus
    B. majors and courses available
    C. preferred subjects
    D. personal reason for attending the lectures in person

2. What does the underlined phrase <u>square one</u> (Line 8, Para. 3) mean?

    A. The first choice.
    B. The learning stage.
    C. The first place.
    D. The starting point.

3. It can be inferred that if one wants to be a teacher, he should choose the major of _____.

    A. accounting
    B. linguistics
    C. engineering
    D. advertising

4. According to Paragraph 5, the person _____ is more likely to get admitted.

   A. who is very efficient and careful in application form but not so with the standard ones
   B. who has few work experiences but makes effort in preparing for the essay writing
   C. who graduated from high school several years ago and has low scores on standardized tests
   D. who has never attended high school but spends a great deal of time preparing for the essay

5. Which of the following statements is correct according to the author?

   A. In the modern technical society, it's becoming easier to attend school online and people should all apply for school online.
   B. Getting your degree is more difficult than paying for it.
   C. Interest is the most important thing in choosing a major.
   D. Balancing working and studying is crucial.

Reading Skills

Patterns of Development

In order to comprehend nonfiction (including textbooks), you'll need the ability to recognize two important features of this kind of writing: patterns of development and transitional elements.

PATTERNS OF DEVELOPMENT				
List of Facts or Details	Examples	Reason—Cause and Effect	Description of a Process	Contrast
Includes factual details to support the main idea.	Uses specific instances of something more general to support the main idea.	Offers reasons (shows causes and effects) that explain why as support for the main idea.	Explains the steps one needs to follow to support the main idea.	Sets two subjects side by side and examines their differences to support the main idea.

These logical processes, which we do all the time in our daily lives, are also present in writing. Called patterns of development, they refer to the internal logic of a passage, the way the writer gets his or her ideas across, the pattern that the writer imposes on his or her material. The choice of the appropriate pattern of development depends on the subject. But your starting point, as the reader, is to recognize that these patterns of development pertain to our thought processes. When looked at this way, you can see that you are already familiar with them.

1. List of facts or details

The pattern of listing facts or listing details is perhaps the simplest one to recognize. Following the main idea, each supporting sentence presents factual evidence to support the main assertion.

2. Examples

An example is a specific instance of something more general. As you saw earlier, nursing and social work are examples of fields involving helping people.

3. Reason—cause and effect

The cause-effect relationship indicates the reasons that explain an effect, which can be a situation, a problem, a trend, in other words, what caused it to occur. In writing, this pattern answers the question "why". Every effect (every situation, every problem, every trend) has at least one cause or reason to explain it—and often multiple causes. First, you need to learn to identify which is the cause and which is the effect.

4. Description of a process

If you wanted to make an omelet for your Sunday morning breakfast, you could follow a cookbook recipe or you could follow your instincts. Either way, you would go through a process, a series of steps that, if followed in order, would produce something edible.

Writers use the process pattern for two primary purposes: (1) to show how to do something, for example, how to make an omelet, how to change a flat tire, or how to burn CDs; or (2) to show how something occurred, for example, how glaciers formed during the Ice Age or how a surfer tackles a big wave.

5. Contrast

How does a Honda differ from a Toyota? How are high school English classes different from college English courses? What are the major differences between the two sports websites espn.com and sportsline.com? When a writer sets two subjects side by side and examines their differences, he or she is using the contrast pattern.

Exercises

Please read the above reading skill of patterns of development and use the guidelines to identify patterns of development of the passage in Short Passage One entitled "Sources of Stress and Anxiety in the Modern World".

Patterns of development:

_____

_____

_____

_____

THINK

Academic Words in Use

Fill in the blanks in the following sentences with the appropriate words provided in the box below. Change the form of the words if necessary.

| appraisal | alternation | self-conscious | prescription | perspective | symptom |
| efficient | technical | positive | appealing | specific | ultimately |

1. An education that aims at getting a student a certain kind of job is a(n) _____ education.

2. This means that we fit our actions to those of other people based on a constant mental process of _____ and interpretation.

3. If you were feeling depressed or overwhelmed, a nice cup of coffee could change your _____.

4. Aerobic exercise is most _____ for weight loss.

5. The natural scenery is always _____ to the imagination with some fresh and unsuspected loveliness.

6. Teenagers are especially _____ and need the confidence that comes from achieving success and knowing that their accomplishments are admired by others.

7. Having made a choice within these limits, we can have certain _____ made.

8. You don't have to give up eating or make the gym your second home to see

long-term _____ effect.

9. Any warning to avoid all stressful events is a(n) _____ for staying away from opportunities as well as trouble.

10. The _____ of jet lag often persist for days while the internal body clock slowly adjusts to the new time zone.

11. The proper schedule for light exposure depends a great deal on _____ travel plan.

12. We forget that they are the guarantee of life systems, on which any built-up area depends _____.

Writing

For this part, you are allowed 30 minutes to read the following paragraph as a guidance and write a well-structured article. You should write at least 120 words but no more than 180 words.

We have approached the topic of growing up from different aspects in this unit. Perhaps the most important realization that an individual can make in his/her quest for personal growth is that there is no single formula that defines the path to personal success. We all have different goals and priorities. We also have different natural strengths and weaknesses that are a part of our inherent personality type. What is your definition of personal growth?

What Is Your Definition of Personal Growth?

Unit 3 — University Culture

Viewing

How to Balance College and Life

About the video clip

This video clip suggests several ways for college students to better balance college and life.

Understanding the video clip

Watch the video clip and fill in the blanks in the table below.

Ways to balance college and life	Details
1. Be realistic	Instead of sleeping 9 hours a day perhaps you'll need to _____ to 7 hours a day, which will probably provide enough energy throughout the day without letting you feel the burnouts. On the other hand, you need to ration the time you spend with your friends and family. The best way to do so is scheduling a fixed time to be with them and dedicate yourself 100% to them. It's not how much time you have available that matters. What matters is what you do with the time you have available. Cutting back on fundamental aspects of your life will really hurt your grades. And if it doesn't hurt your grades right away, it will hurt your body and _____ sooner than you think. Sleepless nights have a mark on your body. On the other hand, depriving yourself of the time spent with your loved ones can hurt and destroy relationships, and in the end of the day you'll find out that those grades aren't worth as much as that.

2. Find some sort of physical activity that helps you manage energy levels	Even running ten minutes a day will do wonders for your _____, letting you cope with high stress levels and the feeling of burnout.
3. Prioritize	Having a heavily crowded schedule just for the sake of it will result in lower grades and the lower ability _____. Big classes and courses that you think you can personally enjoy can also help you on your chosen career path. Try to keep both of those aspects in mind when you're picking subjects for the next semester or else risking signing up for classes that are just _____, and won't even matter when you get your diploma.
4. Find a way to get help	You are not alone in this path and many of your classmates are probably _____. Try to get together and find a way to share some tasks or somehow trade notes and materials to help each other. If you can't attend the lecture for any reason, don't hesitate to ask for _____. Finding a reading group is great to divide huge books into manageable chunks and _____, so you have less reading to do and are able to summarize your part in a better way and then share your summary with your colleagues.
5. Schedule some "me" time	Don't look at your personal space as _____. Try to incorporate at least half an hour with yourself in your busy schedule and stick to it religiously.

Further thoughts

Can you think of other effective ways to balance college and life? List some of them in the table below.

Other ways	Reasons
1. Create a morning routine	1. Create a routine around a daily morning practice, such as meditating or waking up a half-hour early to get work done before ever checking your email. By sticking to this morning after morning, you'll automatically begin your workday on a positive note, with a sense of accomplishment.
2. Set aside quiet time	2. Carving out some time for yourself is essential to stay grounded. Whether you squeeze in time to call a friend or just sit and decompress sans electronic devices, designating uninterrupted time (however short!) to clear your head can work wonders for your mood and will help you to think more clearly when things are moving fast.
...	...

Banked Cloze

Below is a passage with ten blanks. You are required to select one word for each blank from the list of choices given in a word bank following the passage. Read the passage carefully before making your choices. Each choice in the blank is identified by a letter. Please write the corresponding letter for each item in the blanks. You may not use any of the words in the bank more than once.

Mission Statement of Suffolk University[1]

NW: 256 **GL:** 11.3 **AWL percentage:** 8.08%

Keywords: university; mission statement; Suffolk University

Suffolk University[2] is an international institution of traditional and experiential learning. At Suffolk University we are to change lives and 1._____ impact the world. We provide students with superb learning 2._____. Our education leads to extraordinary outcomes for our graduates. Suffolk University is a leader in experiential learning. It has been known nationally and internationally for excellence of teaching. It practically provides students with real-world and global learning opportunities through 3._____ programs.

---

1 From SUFFOLK UNIVERSITY IN BOSTON website.
2 **Suffolk University:** 萨福克大学位于马萨诸塞州波士顿，是一所私立大学，提供全日制和非全日制本科、研究生和法学课程。

We will advance our mission always. We'll try our best to make sure that our students 4. _____ the core competencies to build successful careers in a rapidly changing world. We focus on preparing students for 5. _____ career and success alike. Suffolk University believes in providing a student-centered experience. We build confidence and enable our students to become successful 6. _____ to our world. We create opportunities for students to have an education that will help them achieve their personal goals 7. _____.

We believe in a teacher-scholar model for excellence in teaching. It actively promotes relationships with the world around to 8. _____ knowledge and provide pathways for career development. We engage with our students, alumni, and the broader outer world to promote local and worldwide 9. _____.

Suffolk University values and supports diversity. We faithfully believe that our earth is enriched by people of different backgrounds and cultures. The institution welcomes a(n) 10. _____ student population. African American, Asian, Native American, and women students find a home here since its earliest days. We build a culture of cooperation among different groups. And we encourage free flow of information.

A) damage	B) lifelong	C) connections
D) outstanding	E) strengthen	F) positively
G) exchange	H) gain	I) lovely
J) contributors	K) opportunities	L) negatively
M) diverse	N) inventions	O) effectively

Long Passage

You are going to read a passage with ten statements attached to it. Each statement contains information given in one of the paragraphs. Identify the paragraph from which the information is derived. You may choose a paragraph more than once. Each paragraph is marked with a letter. Please answer the questions by writing the corresponding letter after the statements.

What Are Universities for?[3]

NW: 984 **GL:** 12.4 **AWL percentage:** 6.71% **Keywords:** purpose; university; education

A William von Humboldt did it in 1810, Cardinal Newman did it in 1852 and Lord Robbins did it in 1963. Now recent changes to UK higher education policy have led to strong interest in doing it again—with concern in some quarters that it is not being done enough—that is, defining what universities are for.

B Two events are taking place tomorrow that address the issue. The Centre for Research in the Arts, Social Sciences and Humanities (CRASSH) at the University of Cambridge[4] launches a public lecture series, entitled "The Idea of the University", to mark its 10th anniversary. Then, at the University of East London, a public discussion on

---

[3] From The Guardian website.
[4] University of Cambridge: 剑桥大学，坐落于英国剑桥，在众多领域拥有崇高的学术地位及广泛的影响力，被公认为当今世界最顶尖的高等学府之一。

"University Futures" will consider the purpose of a university education and who should pay for it.

C   Simon Goldhill, director of CRASSH, has lined up speakers including the historian Stefan Collini, astronomer Sir Martin Rees and universities minister David Willetts over the next few weeks. He says the lectures are timely "because government policy is an attempt to change the nature of the university as we have it".

D   Stephen Anderson is the director of the Campaign for Social Science. He is organizing the London debate. He says "there is a sense of living in a real-time experiment", that while the government has created a market economy in higher education it is not yet clear how that constantly moderated market will work. He suggests that potentially far-reaching changes are being made for reasons of financial expediency, without any thought of what their wider effect will be. "What we are all looking for is a greater vision for what the end product might look like," he says. "What is it we are all trying to work to?"

E   For Humboldt, a German philosopher and diplomat, a university was to do with the "whole" community of scholars and students engaged in a common search for truth. For Newman, it was about teaching universal knowledge. For Robbins, an economist commissioned by the government of the time to draw up a report on the future of higher education, universities had four objectives: instruction in skills, promotion of the general powers of the mind, advancement of learning, and transmission of a common culture and common standards of citizenship.

F   For Collini, "one way to begin to think about their distinctiveness is to see them as institutions primarily devoted to extending and deepening human understanding". This, he suggests "is a pretty outrageous idea: no other institutions have this as their primary purpose". He wants to discuss their role "in more fruitful terms than the cliches about 'contributing to economic growth' which currently dominate public debate on the topic".

G   But Mike Rustin, professor of sociology at the University of East London and a speaker at the London discussion, has a problem with this. He says opposition to the government's higher education policy from people such as Collini has so far been expressed in very traditionalist terms—with the idea that a university has an intrinsic value and good.

H   "On the one hand, you have the view of universities as equipping people to earn their living, and on the other hand, a traditional view that universities are about pure learning," he says. "But the students we have here have always seen benefits beyond learning for its own sake."

I   This is also the view of Liam Burns, president of the National Union of Students. "We have really hard evidence to show that students are fairly clear about why they want to go to university—and for the vast majority, it is about getting a better job and having a successful career," he says. "A lot of people say what about learning for learning's sake? I find that problematic. Everyone has a purpose for why they want to learn."

J   Carl Lygo, chief executive of the private higher education provider BPP, agrees, basing his view of university on personal experience. Brought up in a single-parent family and on free school meals, he was the first in his family to attend university, and chose to study law because it offered a clear career path. The fact that more students from his kind of background are now going on to higher education means that the purpose of a university has become more utilitarian he suggests, but he regrets the emphasis now given to its effect on future earning power. "I'm looking forward to when great public universities return to thinking about the wider good," he says.

K   What they all seem to agree is that not all universities are for the same thing, that the "great public universities" are about something very different from BPP. For the philosopher Onora O'Neill, who will give one of the Cambridge lectures, diversity is here to stay, "even if you regard some of its manifestations, such as McDonald's University and company in-house programmes, as probably a bit impertinent". She argues that what is needed is more clarity about precisely what these diverse missions are.

L   As tuition fees begin to differ substantially from one institution to another, the need for clarity about what universities do has been transferred from the government to individual institutions, she argues. Yet the sector has inherited a system that measures them all against the same criteria. Why should inner-city institutions that take large numbers of disadvantaged students be measured on drop-out rates, for example, in the same way as those with a much more traditional student body?

M   What is Willetts's idea of what a university is for? He describes universities first as "one of our great national assets", but adds: "They push forward the frontiers of knowledge. They transform people's lives. And they contribute to the health and wealth of our nation through their deep involvement in wider society and the economy." He also stresses their autonomy. "That is the key to their continuing success and their world-class status."

1. Carl Lygo chose to study law because he was hopping for a bright career in law.
2. CRASSH at the University of Cambridge is going to give a series of lectures.
3. Opinions on the objectives of universities vary from person to person.

4. Changes in the UK higher education policy aroused a strong interest in defining what colleges are for.

5. A professor of sociology at the University of East London is not in favor of the ideas of experts like Collini.

6. There is sufficient evidence to show that college students have a clear purpose for going to college.

7. One of the most distinctive characters of a university is that it is devoted to extending and deepening human understanding.

8. Most college students are hopping to get a better job and have a successful career.

9. University students are always emphasizing benefits beyond learning for its own sake.

10. In the current education system, almost all universities are assessed by the same criteria.

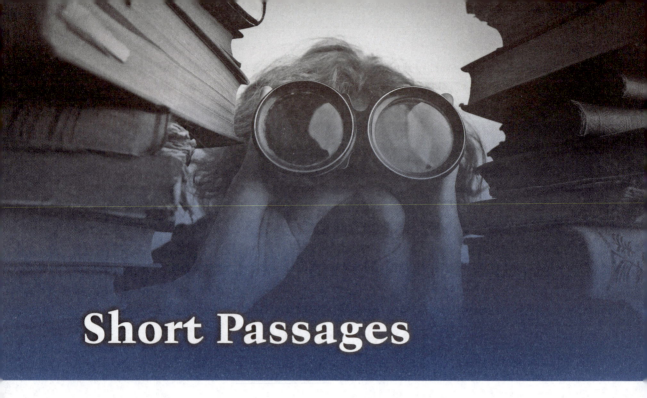

Short Passages

There are two passages in this module. Each passage is followed by some questions or unfinished statements. For each of them there are four choices marked A, B, C, and D. You should decide on the best choice and mark the corresponding letter.

Passage one

College Life Changed Me: I Owe My New Personality to It[5]

NW: 432　**GL:** 11.4　**AWL percentage:** 6.7%　**Keywords:** college life; personality; change

It is said that college life is a phase where one acquires a more independent lifestyle which is certainly different from that students have in school. But for me, in addition to the freedom, college life gave me my feminism, my personality, and the launching pad for my journey ahead. I left my college a year ago, but its essence and learnings are still embedded in what I am today.

I joined Indraprastha College for Women in 2016 as an English Honors student. Why I mention this is because studying English literature at a women's college greatly influenced

---

5　From shethepeople website.

my personality and opinions. The liberating ideas of English literature, the characteristic greeneries and the meditative quietness of my college and its history of feminism together formed a beautiful mess that redefined my identity.

College life for me was not just a change of educational institution. It involved a bigger change of moving from Bihar to Delhi with immense nervousness and feeble hopes. However, when I found a place to live and a good college, I took my first step towards initiating a beautiful change. I became independent, responsible, decisive and ready to adjust in any situation. These are the qualities that I owe to my initial days as a college-going girl.

Since I switched cities, I found it really difficult to adjust to people and their thoughts initially. Hailing from a family where engineering, medical and IAS[6] are the only parameters to measure success and daughters marrying into a good family is the symbol of status I found people at my college liberated. My college life pulled me out of these constraints and put me into a world where there is the freedom to choose, think or say anything I want. I was more of me and less of what society wanted me to be.

Coming from a background that valued society and status over individuality, where sexism was a norm, college life and my course taught me to value myself above everything. Often I felt conflicted between the reality of my college life and my family as if I was living in two different worlds simultaneously. There was always this fear that my college life was just a dream, a break from the world where eventually I will have to go back. But I overcame that fear when I came across people in my college who were facing or had won over the same or worse conflicts. When I interacted with them, their struggles, insight and experience helped me look beyond my conflict and build a perspective and an ambition in life.

1. **Which of the following would the writer of this passage most probably agree?**

   A. My college years changed my personality for the better.

   B. My college was the best because it prepared me for everything to come in the future.

   C. My college provided me with the same kind of freedom as provided in high school.

   D. My college made it possible for me to buy my first iPad.

---

6 IAS: Indian Administrative Service 印度的公务员录用考试

2. According to Paragraph 2, which of the following is NOT true about the writer?

A. She went to a women's college in 2016.

B. She was majoring in English literature in college.

C. She owed her success at college to the help from professors and classmates.

D. She really enjoyed her college years at Indraprastha College for Women.

3. What personalities did the writer develop at college?

A. Nervousness and feeble hopes.

B. Characteristic greeneries and the meditative quietness.

C. Liberating ideas and emerging leadership.

D. Independence, decisiveness and sense of responsibility.

4. Which of the following is a constraint for the writer before she went to college?

A. Switching cities causes difficulty in communication.

B. Personal success is measured by a job in engineering, medical care or IAS.

C. Marrying into a good family is the shortcut for success in life.

D. Freedom to choose, think or say anything is considered supreme.

5. Which of the following is true of the culture the writer was born into?

A. It values society and status.

B. It stresses individuality.

C. It emphasizes equality between men and women.

D. It highlights new insights and experiences.

Passage two

Why I Chose Yale[7]

NW: 373   **GL:** 11.2   **AWL percentage:** 1.59%   **Keywords:** university; Yale; opportunity

It was during the first term of Year 11 (aged 16) that I started to think more seriously about my future.

I had lived in my hometown of Plymouth[8] in the UK for my entire life. It was a nice place to grow up, but it was little more than that, and the thought of studying in the south west of England for longer than I needed to was <u>maddening</u>. I didn't have an exact idea of what I wanted to study at university, let alone for what purpose, but I knew I wanted to do something different. When I expressed this feeling to my teacher, she recommended I think about applying for an American institution.

At first, I knew almost nothing about the American education system, beyond the fact that it was, for lack of a better word, different. All I had was a surface-level idea from Hollywood films and television shows, of shiny, fresh-faced students at places like Harvard and Stanford with a whole world of opportunities at their fingertips.

Slowly, I educated myself. There was plenty of information online about what I needed to do to apply, including advice from current students in YouTube videos and blog posts. I would be required to take the SAT (the American standardized test)[9] and fill out a few more applications than the usual five if I were to apply to British universities. Nevertheless, I felt it was worth a shot. America does, after all, purport to be the land of opportunity. In December 2016, I was accepted by Yale and started studying there nine months later.

My decision to study at Yale instead of going to a British university was not a difficult one. Unlike English universities, where students typically study only one subject for three years, Americans more or less study as many subjects as they want to. Prospective students don't apply to study history or physics, but liberal arts—where students choose classes from a large list, with each class acting like a building block towards a degree. When it comes to extracurricular activities, American universities encourage students to pursue as

---

7 From THE website.
8 Plymouth: 普利茅斯，位于英国英格兰西南区域德文郡，东北 310 公里达英国首都伦敦。普利茅斯是英国皇家海军所在地，也是 16 世纪至 19 世纪英国人出海的港口。
9 SAT: 也称"美国高考"，是由美国大学理事会（College Board）主办的一项标准化、以笔试形式进行的高中毕业生学术能力水平考试。其成绩是世界各国高中毕业生申请美国高等教育院校入学资格及奖学金的重要学术能力参考指标。

many interests as possible, to make connections with others and to have fun doing so. This massively appealed to me.

1. Which of the following account of Plymouth is NOT true according to the first two paragraphs?

   A. Before I went to U.S., I mainly lived there.
   B. It is a good place for a man to stay for his entire life.
   C. It is a nice place for children to grow up.
   D. It is the place where the writer of this passage had been staying for 16 years.

2. The underlined word "maddening" (Line 3, Para. 2) can best be replaced by?

   A. Discouraging.
   B. Disadvantageous.
   C. Exclusive.
   D. Imaginary.

3. What did the writer of this passage think of American universities before he came to the U.S.?

   A. American universities are very different from one another.
   B. American university students favor Hollywood films.
   C. There are all kinds of opportunities for students in American universities.
   D. One needs to have good hand writing to get permitted into an American university.

4. Which of the following is NOT the way the writer of this passage got the information needed to know about application?

   A. He went to the library to read books about American universities.
   B. He went online to check related information.
   C. He viewed YouTube videos.
   D. He came to blog posts for advice.

5. **There are a lot of differences between American universities and British ones EXCEPT _____.**

A. Students in an American university learn as many subjects as they like, while those in a British university can only learn one.

B. Students in an American university learn liberal arts, while those in a British university may learn history or physics.

C. Students in an American university choose their classes to learn in, while those in a British university may not have much choice.

D. Students in an American university are usually granted a degree, while those in a British university are not.

Reading Skills

Using Examples to Support Claims

Usually when a writer makes a claim, it needs to be supported. One way to do this is by providing concrete examples. These may (but not always) be introduced with a phrase such as "for example", or "for instance", "like", and "such as". In Short Passage Two, the writer makes the claim that he began to look for information himself. This is supported by mentioning advice from current students in YouTube videos/blog posts, and the requirement to take SAT and fill out a few applications.

Exercises

Please read the above reading skill of using examples to support claims and follow the guidelines to support the topic sentence by giving sufficient examples.

Computers can help people in different ways. _____

_____

_____

Whatever you are doing, you may find computers a useful aid.

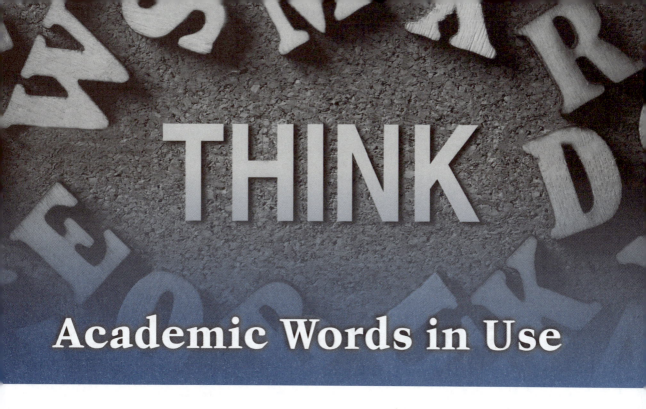

Academic Words in Use

Fill in the blanks in the following sentences with the appropriate words provided in the box below. Change the form of the words if necessary.

aspect	assignment	available	colleague	energy	focus
goal	grade	lecture	mental	schedule	stress

1. Finally, as a professor, I am aware that not every _____ can be a Nobel winner.
2. "We found that women as well as men have lower levels of _____ at work than at home", writes one of the researchers.
3. It takes a while to judge complex _____ of personality, like neuroticism or open-mindedness.
4. A large number of the homeless have serious _____ problems.
5. If you're not sure, ask for honest feedback from trusted friends, _____ and professionals.
6. The meeting was held according to _____.
7. If the district finds homework to be unimportant to students, it should move to reduce or eliminate the _____.
8. For first-generation college students, their _____ are lower and their dropout rates are higher.
9. If you are surrounded by problems and cannot stop thinking about the past, try to _____ on the present moment.
10. Don't waste your time and _____ on trifles.
11. But science does provide us with the best _____ guide to the future.
12. Get the support of professionals and share with them your _____ and attempts.

Writing

For this part, you are allowed 30 minutes to read the following paragraph and continue writing to make it a well-structured article. You should write at least 120 words but no more than 180 words.

My View on the Postgraduate Craze

Every year, millions of college students sit in for the postgraduate entrance examination. More and more students have regarded the pursuing of a master degree as an indispensable part of their education. What is to account for their enthusiasm for a postgraduate diploma?

Unit 4 Lifestyles I Like

Viewing

Maintaining a Healthy Balanced Lifestyle

About the video clip

This video clip discusses 5 things we should think about for leading a healthy balanced lifestyle.

Understanding the video clip

Watch the video clip and fill in the blanks in the table below.

Suggestions	Details
1. A nutritious breakfast	Kicking off the day with a nutritious breakfast is a good place to start. Why? When we _____, our body has been without food for a number of hours, so we need to eat something to give us the _____. From walking and talking through two critical functions such as breathing and pumping blood around our body, even thinking requires energy, so breakfast and food generally is pretty important. There are other benefits too. Evidence shows that those who eat breakfast _____ than those who skip it. And children who eat breakfast concentrate more and perform better at school.

2. Right amount of sugar	Our brain requires around 130 grams of glucose, which is a type of sugar per day _____. You'll find glucose in all sorts of foods from fruit and vegetables to honey. So for a healthy start to your day and to get that early morning energy boost, how about enjoying some porridge with raisins or maybe a small glass of orange juice and _____. Today, more and more of us are eating on-the-go than ever before. This can make it more difficult to _____ we're eating as we go with the added extras or grabbing a coffee with our sandwich.
3. Nutritional labels	Nutritional labels can help us _____ how we're doing. They include lots of useful information from the calorie content to the different ingredients including the amount of total sugars. Did you know that _____ sugars our bodies do not distinguish between them whether natural or added in the home or used in manufacturing? So the sucrose in an apple is broken down _____ as the sucrose in your sugar bowl. As our energy levels dip through the day, it can be tempting to reach for a mid-afternoon snack. Snacks can make up to 20% of our daily calorie intake. So think about how snacks can complement the other foods you've eaten through the day. It's also worth thinking about how your snacks can help you get one of your five a day.
4. Look after yourself	A couple of ways to look after yourself includes _____ what you're eating and leading an active lifestyle. The UK government recommends 150 minutes of moderate exercise or 75 minutes of more vigorous exercise for adults each week. As you approach dinner, _____ to think about the food you've eaten through the day. No single food or drink contains all the essential nutrients your body needs. Also think about the number of calories you've consumed and how active you've been.
5. Be careful with drinks	Finally, don't forget that drinks also count towards your daily calorie allowance so that small glass of white wine or a pint of beer shouldn't be forgotten when totting up _____ for the day.

Further thoughts

The topic of lifestyles has triggered a continuous wave of animated discussion over its being healthy or unhealthy. List some of them in the table below.

Unhealthy lifestyles	Healthy lifestyles
1. Eat too much meat and a few vegetables.	1. Eat a lot of fresh fruits and vegetables.
2. Stay up late.	2. Have a good hight sleep.
...	...

Banked Cloze

Below is a passage with ten blanks. You are required to select one word for each blank from the list of choices given in a word bank following the passage. Read the passage carefully before making your choices. Each choice in the blank is identified by a letter. Please write the corresponding letter for each item in the blanks. You may not use any of the words in the bank more than once.

The Best Way to Find Balance in Your Life[1]

NW: 362 **GL:** 5.6 **AWL percentage:** 4.64% **Keywords:** balance; life; unstable

"How do you find work and life balance?" I get asked this question very often, 1._____ when facilitating workshops. No matter the topic, the notion of balance comes up all the time. People believe my life is balanced and want to know how I do it.

Life balance is a mirage—the closer you think you get, the further away it goes. "Stop aiming for it, and you'll find balance," I tell them. Maybe you feel 2._____— that's how most people initially react when I provide this answer. They were 3._____ five productivity tips, not a play on words. However, when I make them go through some exercises, they realize this simple statement has more profound 4._____.

Balance is not something we can get; it's a state of mind. It's the realization that life

---

1 From Psychology Today website.

is not 5._____ but in constant motion. Life is almost like riding a bicycle. "Freedom without discipline is foolish, discipline without freedom is insanity," said Ilona Mialiko. But what does it mean to lead a well-balanced life? Why does balance feel like an elusive 6._____?

The paradox of balance is that, the more we 7._____ it, the more things seem to fall apart. Our worries make us worry more. The word "balance" is both a noun and a verb. No wonder we 8._____ to find it! Balance is an even distribution of weight enabling someone or something to remain upright and steady. When we see "balance" as a noun, we believe it will bring stability to our lives.

Balance is 9._____ things into harmony. It's not something that you can get, but something that you continually do. Life is a game in which you are continually juggling many balls in the air. Albert Einstein said, "Life is like riding a bicycle. To keep your balance, you must keep moving." Life is a balancing act—everything is in constant motion.

Things will never go your way; 10._____ events will always show up uninvited. Your boss will add a new meeting to your busy schedule. A friend will call you last minute to cancel dinner plans. Learn to adapt to the moment rather than rigidly sticking to plans.

A) struggle	B) pursue	C) success
D) implications	E) movements	F) stable
G) bringing	H) especially	I) unexpected
J) expecting	K) concept	L) disappointed
M) taking	N) possible	O) really

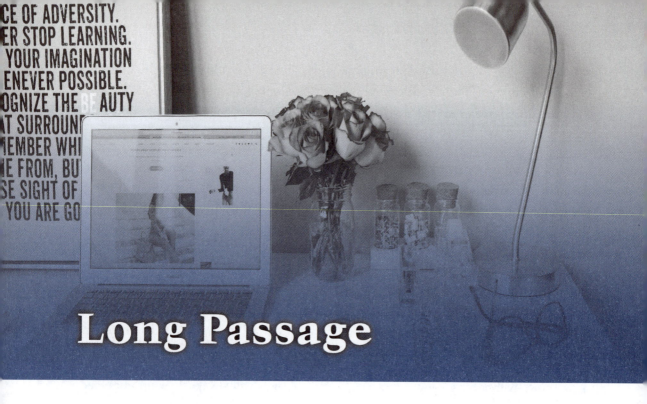

Long Passage

You are going to read a passage with ten statements attached to it. Each statement contains information given in one of the paragraphs. Identify the paragraph from which the information is derived. You may choose a paragraph more than once. Each paragraph is marked with a letter. Please answer the questions by writing the corresponding letter after the statements.

Should You Strive for Work/Life Balance? The History of the Personal & Professional Divide[2]

NW: 1,097　**GL:** 10.5　**AWL percentage:** 6.24%　**Keywords:** life; balance; divide

A　　Tips for reaching this coveted state-of-being range from the physical (like exercising) to the psychological (like meditating and mentally "disconnecting" from work) to the sociological (like scheduling all of your outside-of-work interactions/activities with friends and family).

B　　Don't get me wrong. Many of these tips can be helpful. Implementing them could yield you a happier, more fulfilling life—both in terms of your work life and your personal life. But you see, this is where the term gets confusing. "Work/life" balance implies that your work (your job or your career) and your life (your being or your

---

2　From thinkgrowth website.

existence) are on par with each other.

C   "The problem with work-life balance is that it suggests there is a trade-off—that one side must be 'up' and the other one 'down,' like a weighing scale that has two sides to it," Jappreet Sethi, CEO of Ideak Katalyst, wrote on LinkedIn in June of 2014.

D   He continued, "Using the word 'balance' suggests that the two aspects are completely separate from one another and are at odds, that when you are at work you're not really living." To be sure, this is by no means a novel criticism of the concept. In fact, at HubSpot, we often encourage "work/life" balance in employees. The goal of this article is to dive into the terminology, uncover the challenges, and explore the way in which the concept shapes our experiences.

E   Of course, many of us don't interpret the "life" in "work/life" balance to mean our actual lives; what we really mean is our lifestyles, our leisure time. And that's precisely what the concept used to be called: work/leisure balance. Up until the 1980s, nobody talked about "work/life" balance, they talked about "work/leisure balance." And that concept—balancing work and leisure—goes back to the days of Plato[3] and Aristotle[4]. (More on that later.)

F   So, why the change in terminology? And if we really mean "lifestyle" nowadays when we're talking about "work/life" balance, why don't we say "lifestyle"? Are we that lazy that we need to shorten it? (I mean, I know I am that lazy. But I can't speak for everyone.) Semantics aside, the notion of "work/life" balance is confounding (and potentially detrimental) on a number of other levels.

G   As Boris Groysberg and Robin Abrahams noted in the March 2014 issue of the Harvard Business Review: "'Work/life' balance is at best an elusive ideal and at worst a complete myth, today's senior executives will tell you." So, could striving for some imaginary, idealistic sense of balance end up having negative repercussions on your life? That's what we'll be exploring in the paragraphs to come.

H   But first, I want to take a step back and review the history and etymology of "work/life" balance. We've glanced over this briefly already, but having a better understanding of how the concept (and terminology) has evolved over time will help us to better evaluate its modern incarnation.

I   Time ago, there are no jobs… at least not in the usual sense of the word. But there is still work—people must hunt, forage, and fish for food in order to survive. (And

---

3 Plato: 柏拉图（古希腊哲学家）
4 Aristotle: 亚里士多德（古希腊著名思想家）

of course, they must take care of their children in order to ensure the survival of the species.) Despite their lack of technology (or perhaps, because of it), our hunter/gatherer ancestors probably spent fewer hours working than we do today, and spent more time on things like music, art, storytelling, and getting busy in the bedroom or cave, or whatever. It's also unclear whether our ancestors actually made a distinction between work and leisure. For them, it probably all just fell under the umbrella of "life".

J   The First Agricultural Revolution, also known as the Neolithic Revolution, made it possible for many of our foraging forebears to settle down. Growing crops and raising livestock assured a steady food supply, which meant people didn't have to rely on hunting and gathering to survive. "Farming" soon replaced "spear-throwing" as the most popular skill on LinkedIn at the time.

K   But as populations began growing around these steady food supplies, not everyone could be a farmer, and people who weren't farmers needed stuff to do, apparently. That's when job specialization started to take off. For the first time ever, people began to have individual jobs. In addition to farmers, there were clay pot makers, builders, carpenters, soldiers, and so on.

L   For the first time ever, you could go up to someone and ask, "What do you do for a living?" and the answer would be something other than: "Survive." This is, arguably, the time when a person's work became more clearly aligned with a person's identity. And when the distinction between "work time" and "leisure time" became more pronounced. Aristotle first explores the notion of balancing work and leisure in his works *Nicomachean Ethics* and *Politics*. Here's a quote from the latter:

M   "The whole of life is further divided into two parts, business and leisure, war and peace, and of actions some aim at what is necessary and useful, and some at what is honorable. And the preference given to one or the other class of actions must necessarily be like the preference given to one or other part of the soul and its actions over the other; there must be war for the sake of peace, business for the sake of leisure, things useful and necessary for the sake of things honorable."

N   Ultimately, however, Aristotle's interpretation of leisure wasn't a very egalitarian one. He contended that the majority of people worked not for the sake of their own leisure, but so that a minority of educated people could enjoy it and thus have time to devote themselves to "higher" pursuits.

O   As Italian philosopher Adriano Tilgher noted in his 1931 book, *Work: What It Has Meant to Men Through the Ages*, Aristotle's advice for achieving a good or moral life was to "have the hard, troublesome work of transforming raw material for the satisfaction of our needs done by a part—the majority—of men, in order that the minority, the elite, might engage in pure exercise of the mind—art, philosophy, politics."

P Working at this time (specifically manual labor) wasn't something to be proud of. In fact, the Greek word for work, *ponos*, was derived from the Latin word, *poena*, which meant "sorrow". After centuries of people viewing work as essentially a necessary evil, the "work/life" scale began to tilt in the direction of work.

1. Work/life balance is taken as a complete myth by some experts.
2. "Life" in "work/life" balance actually refers to our lifestyles.
3. Understanding the history of work/life balance helps us know it better.
4. When population grew, people began to have individual jobs of many kinds.
5. According to Aristotle, most people worked so that the educated ones could have more time to do great things.
6. The idea of work/life balance has been criticized.
7. The First Agricultural Revolution made it possible for the primitive men to settle down somewhere.
8. Aristotle was the one who first explored the concept of balancing work and leisure.
9. The term "work/life balance" bears the implication that work and life are of equal importance.
10. Our ancestors most probably worked for shorter time than we do today.

Short Passages

There are two passages in this module. Each passage is followed by some questions or unfinished statements. For each of them there are four choices marked A, B, C, and D. You should decide on the best choice and mark the corresponding letter.

Passage one

Work-Life Balance Is a Myth. Do This Instead[5]

NW: 485 **GL:** 8.8 **AWL percentage:** 4.09% **Keywords:** work; life; balance

If you think about it, work-life balance is a strange aspiration for a fulfilling life. Balance is about stasis: If our lives were ever in balance—parents happy, kids taken care of, work working—then our overriding thought would be to shout "Nobody move!" and pray all would stay perfect forever. This false hope is made worse by the categories themselves. They imply that work is bad, and life is good; we lose ourselves in work but find ourselves in life; we survive work, but live life. And so the challenge, we are told, is to balance the heaviness of work with the lightness of life.

Yet work is not the opposite of life. It is instead a part of life—just as family is, as

---

5 From TIME website.

are friends and community and hobbies. All of these aspects of living have their share of wonderful, uplifting moments and their share of moments that drag us down. The same is true of work, yet when we think of it as an inherent bad in need of a counterweight, we lose sight of the possibility for better.

It seems more useful, then, to not try to balance the unbalanceable, but to treat work the same way you do life: By maximizing what you love. Here's what we mean.

Consider why two people doing exactly the same work seem to gain strength and joy from very different moments. When we interviewed several anesthesiologists, we found that while their title and job function are identical, the thrills and chills they feel in their job are not. One said he loved the thrill of holding each patient hovering at that one precise point between life and death, while he shuddered at the "pressure" of helping each patient get healthy once the operation was complete.

Another said she loved the bedside conversations before the operation, and the calm sensitivity required to bring a sedated patient gently back to consciousness without the panic that afflicts many patients. Another was drawn mostly to the intricacies of the anesthetic mechanism itself and has dedicated herself to defining precisely how each drug does what it does. Each one of us, for no good reason other than the clash of our chromosomes, draws strength from different activities, situations, moments and interactions.

Think of your life's many different activities as threads. Some are black, some are grey and some are white. But some of these activities appear to be made of a different substance. These activities contain all the tell-tale signs of love: Before you do them, you find yourself looking forward to them; while you're doing them, time speeds up and you find yourself in flow; and after you've done them, you feel invigorated. These are your red threads, and research by the Mayo Clinic suggests that doctors who weave the fabric of their life with at least 20% red threads are significantly less likely to experience burnout.

1. **What's the writer's attitude to our common belief about work-life balance?**

   A. Positive.
   B. Supportive.
   C. Negative.
   D. Indifferent.

2. Which of the following can best replace the underlined word "uplifting" (Line 3, Paragraph 2) ?

   A. Inspiring.

   B. Discouraging.

   C. Uneasy.

   D. Difficult.

3. Why two people doing exactly the same work can gain strength and joy from very different moments?

   A. Because some are anesthesiologists, but others are physicians.

   B. Because the thrills and chills they feel in their job are different.

   C. Because they have different titles and job functions.

   D. Because they are not good at helping patients get healthy after operations.

4. What does the underlined word "afflicts" (Line 3, Paragraph 5) most probably mean?

   A. Effects.

   B. Efforts.

   C. Affords.

   D. Affects.

5. Which of the following would the writer agree?

   A. It's best for us to pick up the activities that we really love to do in our work.

   B. It's best for us to have furniture of different color in our house.

   C. It's best for us to go to see a doctor for advice when we are not healthy.

   D. It's best for us to take seriously the conclusions from researchers.

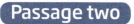

Our Unhealthy Obsession with Entertainment[6]

NW: 367 **GL:** 9.3 **AWL percentage:** 5.15%
Keywords: entertainment; addiction; American society

I remember Laura Bush told a Moscow audience that she believes American children are addicted to television very much during her trip to Russia and France two years ago.

The First Lady[7] will get no argument here. However, I would suggest that TV is only the delivery system for a much more pervasive addiction. The compulsive habit that appeals to not only children, but also adults, is not tangible per se. It is a concept. The irresistible force that now saturates American society is entertainment.

There is little about life in the United States that is not tainted by the insatiable desire to be amused. GameBoys, Walkmans, and DVDs provide fun and diversion that is portable. Cell phones and PDAs now come with games as standard equipment.

Americans pursue electronic pastimes via television and computer. The Internet, which helped usher in the information age, is now primarily used for amusement—much of which is unseemly. And movies are available 24 hours a day, 7 days a week, 365 days a year via cable.

Professional sport has even been affected by America's entertainment addiction. Once the games themselves were amusement enough. Not any more. I was treated to an NBA contest this past season. There I encountered non-stop entertainment. During breaks in the action there were contests, souvenir give-a-ways, dancing girls, and video replays. It was dizzying.

Politics is now dominated by entertainment in some way. A candidate's image has become more important than a substantive platform. Televised debates are nothing more than rehearsed sound bites and staged spin. A political pundit recently declared that a particular individual would make a good candidate because he makes the public feel good.

The church is even being tempted by society's quest to be entertained. Once a local fellowship was evaluated by its commitment to biblical truth. No more. Many who file in and out of houses of worship now expect a service to flow with flawless musical

---

6 From *English Language Learning* by Boggs K.
7 First Lady: 第一夫人（国家元首的妻子）

presentations and engaging messages peppered with humor. Conviction must now contend with amusement.

There is little in American society that has not been tainted by entertainment addiction. Perhaps we should consider the song "Let Me Entertain You" as our new national anthem.

1. **What is the writer's purpose in mentioning the First Lady Laura Bush in the first paragraph?**

   A. To show that political figures like watching TV.
   B. To show that Laura was rather good at speeches as First Lady.
   C. To prove that Americans have good life habits.
   D. To prove that Americans are now obsessed with entertainment.

2. **Which of the following is NOT a means of pastime for Americans?**

   A. GameBoys, Walkmans and DVDs.
   B. Cell phones and PADs.
   C. Google Glass and robots.
   D. Televisions and computers.

3. **Which of the following statement is true according to Paragraphs 5 and 6?**

   A. Sport today is as good as they were in the past.
   B. Professional sport and politics are heavily affected by entertainment.
   C. Last year, the writer himself took part in an NBA contest.
   D. Students are offered more online interaction with their professors.

4. **What is true of religious service in a church according to the passage?**

   A. A computer file is a must.
   B. The purpose is to get rid of temptations.
   C. It is highly under the influence of people's desire for entertainment.
   D. It is liked by those who favor flawless music and humous messages.

5. By saying "we should consider the song 'Let Me Entertain You' as our new national anthem" (Paragraph 8), the writer means _____.

A. the original national anthem is not good enough and should be replaced

B. we have been paying too much attention to the interest of our nation

C. almost everything in the country is affected by entertainment, which is unreasonable

D. things out of date should be definitely taken away

Reading Skills

Drawing an Inference and a Conclusion

Careful and thoughtful readers always think about what they are reading, trying to interpret the ideas presented in a reading passage. In doing so they are able to draw inferences and conclusions based on what the author tells them.

In order to draw reasonable inferences and conclusions, you always have to return to the selection, read the appropriate passage again, and think about the writer's words and what they suggest. You need to do the following:

1. Look up the meanings of any unfamiliar words and consider the definitions in context.

2. Think about the possibilities of interpretation by examining the writers' words and phrases.

3. Look carefully at the way the statement is worded. Then return to the passage and locate the pertinent passage. Test the statement for accuracy.

4. Remember that inferences are statements of probability, not facts. They proceed from facts, but they are not facts themselves.

5. Consider what each sentence says about the common topic.

6. Ask yourself what general thought or idea emerges when you put all of those

individual pieces of information together.

7. Think of the idea that emerges as the author's implied main idea and the purpose of the passage.

Exercises

Please read the above reading skill of drawing an inference and a conclusion and use the guidelines to work out the writer's purpose in writing the passage in Short Passage Two entitled "Our Unhealthy Obsession with Entertainment".

Purpose: In writing the passage the writer intends to _____

_____

_____

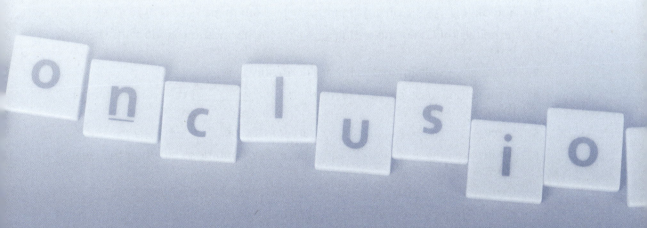

THINK

Academic Words in Use

Fill in the blanks in the following sentences with the appropriate words provided in the box below. Change the form of the words if necessary.

| challenge | despite | editor | individual | issue | majority |
| philosopher | physical | previous | rely | survive | job |

1. You can't _____ on any figures you get from them.
2. Although this is an interesting _____, it has nothing to do with the topic today.
3. Of the six people injured in the accident, only two _____.
4. While all of these countries face their own _____, there are a number of things in common.
5. Some _____ experience is necessary for this job.
6. As anyone knows, a person's early life and its conditions are often the greatest gift to a(n) _____.
7. Certain _____ have gone away for good because of machines.
8. As the Chinese _____ Chuang Tzu once said: "Happiness is the absence of striving for happiness."
9. _____ old age, she is still learning to drive.
10. The _____ benefits of exercise can be divided into three aspects.
11. The _____ of people seem to prefer printed books to e-books.
12. "This indicates there is a real personal responsibility," says Roxanne Stone, _____ in chief at Barna Group.

Writing

For this part, you are allowed 30 minutes to read the following paragraph and continue writing to make it a well-structured article. You should write at least 120 words but no more than 180 words.

Live a Healthy Life

A healthy lifestyle is not only a way to avoid risks, but also a chance to live well and happily. Once you choose to live a healthy life, it lasts all your life. It not only helps you live longer and better but also let you be less prone to sickness and diseases. A healthy lifestyle is the kind of lifestyle that we should all strive for.

Unit 5 — Emotion & Interaction

Viewing

Discipline Your Emotion

About the video clip

This video clip discusses how to control your emotion.

Understanding the video clip

Watch the video clip and fill in the blanks in the table below.

1. Don't waste your time in other people's life.	1. We need to believe the dots will connect the road, will give your the _____ to _____ your heart. Don't let the _____ of others' _____ drown out your own _____.
2. Work will be a great part of life.	2. Your work is gonna fill a large part of your life and the only way to be _____ is to do what you _____, and the only way to do great work is to love what you do.
3. Don't give up easily.	3. Most people give up on themselves easily. You know the _____. The real challenge of growth _____ and _____ comes when you get knocked down.

4. Don't be afraid of fear.	4. Fear can hold you back from doing something that you know _____ that you're _____ doing, but it will paralyze you.
5. Be the master of your emotion.	5. Don't allow your emotions to control you. We are _____ but you want to begin to _____. It's not easy. If it were in fact easy, everybody would do it. But if you're serious, you'll go all out. You're standing up for your _____. You're standing up for _____. You're standing up for _____.

Further thoughts

There is a fierce debate on whether we should hide our emotion in public. List the pros and cons for not hiding one's emotion in public in the table below.

Pros	Cons
1. As a person, I have the right to express my emotion.	1. Personal emotion is a private thing.
2. Only after I release the bad emotion, I can feel happy.	2. Don't let other people see your worst side, it is a good way to protect yourself.
…	…

Unit 5   Emotion & Interaction

Banked Cloze

Below is a passage with ten blanks. You are required to select one word for each blank from the list of choices given in a word bank following the passage. Read the passage carefully before making your choices. Each choice in the blank is identified by a letter. Please write the corresponding letter for each item in the blanks. You may not use any of the words in the bank more than once.

First Impression[1]

NW: 249　GL: 9.3　AWL percentage: 6.43%
Keywords: first impression; psychological factors; communication skill

Here is an interesting fact: The average person forms a first impression of someone in less than 30 seconds. First impression are the 1._____ someone has about you when you meet for the first time. What is your smile telling the other person? What is the way you 2._____ saying about you? These factors can make a difference in the way the person thinks about you.

Handshakes, facial expressions, and general appearance help to create first impressions. People are 3._____ forming these impressions of others. We do not make these impressions consciously. They are largely 4._____. However, they tend to be extremely difficult to change.

---

1 From *Grammar and Beyond(3)* by Blass L, Iannuzzi S, Savage A & Reppen R.

Some psychologists today are researching the factors that influence how people react to others. For example, psychologist Brian Nosek is currently using a collection of tests known as the IAT, or Implicit Association Test[2] for his research. These tests are helping to reveal our thinking processes, both conscious and subconscious, as we 5._____ our impressions of others. 6._____, Nosek is investigating our use of stereotypes and attitudes about others in forming first impressions.

Each test measures what happens while people are making judgments. The results demonstrate that people have stereotypes, and that these stereotypes 7._____ their first impressions. For example, both young people and old people tend to associate the word 8."_____" with pictures of young people.

Since first impressions influence what a person thinks about you to a great 9._____, it is important to always do your 10._____ to make a good first impression.

A) best	B) dress	C) control
D) opinions	E) words	F) good
G) seldom	H) personality	I) influence
J) constantly	K) subconscious	L) specifically
M) change	N) degree	O) form

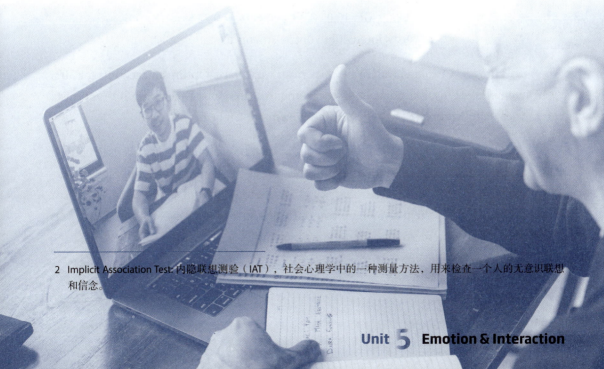

2 Implicit Association Test: 内隐联想测验（IAT），社会心理学中的一种测量方法，用来检查一个人的无意识联想和信念。

Unit 5　Emotion & Interaction

Long Passage

You are going to read a passage with ten statements attached to it. Each statement contains information given in one of the paragraphs. Identify the paragraph from which the information is derived. You may choose a paragraph more than once. Each paragraph is marked with a letter. Please answer the questions by writing the corresponding letter after the statements.

Why You Shouldn't Always Look on the Bright Side[3]

NW: 822 **GL:** 10.0 **AWL percentage:** 9.23 %
Keywords: interaction; optimism; understanding

A Optimism is a valued trait in the American workplace. Optimism accounts for 30% of an employee's inspiration at work, according to a survey by Leadership IQ. Optimists may deal with workplace stress better, and they may even be healthier.

B But having a relentlessly sunny attitude can also be a problem, says licensed clinical psychologist Robyn L. Gobyn, assistant professor at the University of Illinois Urbana-Champaign and author of the *Doing My Work Therapy Journal*. When your optimism clouds your view to the point where you can't see—or worse, deny—real problems, you could be causing more problems than you're solving.

---

3 From FASTCOMPANY website.

C   "What I tell (my clients) is that I want them to look at the world through clear-colored glasses, not rose-colored glasses," she says. "It's possible to cross the line and be too optimistic."

D   When optimism turns into denial—a situation experts such as Gobyn call "toxic positivity"—it can wreak havoc on workplace relationships. So, understanding the difference between the two is important.

Understanding the difference

E   Optimism means that you expect or anticipate positive outcomes, or perhaps you expect the best from others. But when you are repeatedly "blindsided" by outcomes, you may be unrealistically optimistic, says organizational psychology consultant David Shar. When your expectations are repeatedly not matching the data and you're not prepared for a negative outcome, you might have crossed the line, he says.

F   "You keep saying, 'This thing is going to work out, or coronavirus is going to be over next week,' and that doesn't happen," he says. If you are denying real problems in favor of happy outcomes, you need to take a closer look at how you're processing data, he says. A 2017 study in the journal *Consciousness and Cognition* says that, while it's difficult to say for certain if someone has unrealistic optimism, one indicator is if they update their beliefs based on new information. If they're only looking at the positive information and updating beliefs with an optimistic bias, there may be a problem.

What's so bad about being too positive?

G   Of all the issues to worry about, why is toxic positivity a big deal? Mostly because of the impact it has on your team, says therapist Lauren Cook, author of *Name Your Story: How to Talk Openly about Mental Health while Embracing Wellness*. Your unrealistic optimism may be creating barriers to their success.

H   Gobyn agrees. When you're on the path to toxic positivity, you may be invalidating your emotions and those of the people around you. Instead of acknowledging that there may be challenges or difficulties and preparing for them, people who are in the thick of toxic positivity simply deny the potential for problems. "I want them to see the fullness of their potential, and to notice that, yes, this is a challenging moment. And yes, I'm having difficult emotions right now. And also, I can do hard things," she says. Looking at your past realistically and reminding yourself of the hard things you've overcome before can give you both insight and strength.

I   Your team members may also feel like you're gaslighting them, Cook says. Someone may be sharing difficult information or emotions with you, and if you respond simply,

"Oh, it's going to be fine," you could be invalidating someone's experience. And that can erode trust, diminish your credibility as a leader, and lead to resentment and disengagement, she says.

J Cook, who also wrote a book on happiness, has first-hand experience with the matter. "My original brand was the sunny girl. I would literally wear a yellow dress when I would go out and speak," she says. But her research on happiness has revealed that people are actually happier and less likely to engage in behaviors that obscure emotions when they're living authentically. "I think it's the reason why a lot of us engage in unhealthy numbing behaviors, because we're not learning how to handle difficult, painful emotions. And that work is honestly just as important as learning how to be happy," she says.

Guarding against toxic positivity

K So, how can you prevent slipping into toxic positivity while still maintaining your optimistic outlook? It starts with looking at the data, Shar says. We all have confirmation bias, he says. But if we work at looking at circumstances and information objectively and allow for the possibility that things might not turn out the way we expect, we can prepare for those outcomes.

L Gobyn says that turning into our emotions is also essential. "Our emotions are like those alerts that come on in our car, like that the tire pressure is low. And we can definitely ignore them and keep driving. But at some point, like the tire is going to be flat, or there's no oil, and the current system won't be functioning," she says. When you feel that sense that things might not be alright, check in with yourself and figure out why.

M Shar says it's also important to surround yourself with people who may be more objective or who have a different outlook and truly listen to what they have to say. "If you know that you tend to be overly optimistic, you've got to get a realist in there—somebody who's a little bit maybe more critical, who's going to challenge you, and you have to make sure to give that person a voice," he says. This not only informs your outlook, but it also makes your team members feel heard and can cultivate greater trust.

1. People haven't learned how to deal with the negative emotions, so they put themselves in an indifferent style. ☐
2. Someone's overpositive emotion will do harm to the team's achievements. ☐
3. Leadership IQ found that optimism made up for parts of the employee's motivation. ☐

4. People who always enjoy the favorable information and deny the opposite one might be involved in an imaginary optimism. ☐

5. People need to keep a great balance between the expectation and the reality. ☐

6. When optimism blinded one's way, it could produce more serious problems. ☐

7. People only have optimism instead of enough preparation for the result. They need to be careful about it. ☐

8. Optimism will have a negative effect on workplace if it changes into denial. ☐

9. Taking care of the emotions is just like taking care of the cars. ☐

10. Don't deny the past. The failures can also offer the power to overcome today's difficulties. ☐

Short Passages

There are two passages in this module. Each passage is followed by some questions or unfinished statements. For each of them there are four choices marked A, B, C, and D. You should decide on the best choice and mark the corresponding letter.

Passage one

People of All Ages[4]

NW: 308 **GL:** 9.7 **AWL percentage:** 5.19% **Keywords:** children; senior; social life

Do you know that in the United States, over 25 percent of senior citizens (people over 65) live alone? Without enough friends and family nearby, seniors are at risk of depression. This is a serious problem. Studies show that people with depression are more likely to have other health problems as well.

Now, many communities are trying to find a solution to this problem. Providence Mount St. Vincent, a retirement home near Seattle, Washington, has recently launched an intergenerational program[5]. Over 400 senior citizens live at Providence Mount St. Vincent,

---

4　From *World Link 3* by Douglas N & Morgan J.
5　intergenerational program: 代际计划

and over 40 children from a few months old to age five go to daycare there. The children spend the day there with the senior citizens while workers look on.

An intergenerational program like the one at Providence Mount St. Vincent has clear benefits. For the older people, their social life improves; they read to and play games with the children, and encourage them in a wide range of other activities. Being involved with the children makes the seniors feel useful and happy, and if they feel happy, their overall mental and physical health may improve.

The children also benefit from the program. They have an enthusiastic and patient group of people to play with in a safe environment. Some of the seniors are also disabled, and studies also show that if children <u>are exposed to</u> people with disabilities at a young age, they will learn to be more tolerant and understanding of people like this.

Providence Mount St. Vincent was even featured in a documentary film called *Present Perfect*. As families of both the young and the old see the benefits, intergenerational programs are expanding. The film's message is starting to spread: Even if the very young and the very old don't have a shared past or future, their shared present can be perfect.

1. **The senior have a higher risk of depression because _____.**
   A. they have a lonely character
   B. their friends and relatives live far away from them
   C. they don't want to share their opinions with others
   D. they refuse to talk with other people

2. **The senior took part in many activities with the children including _____.**
   A. studying
   B. reading and playing games
   C. flying kites
   D. doing sports

3. **The children also benefit from the program, because _____.**
   A. the environment is safe
   B. people with them are patient and enthusiastic
   C. it will help them have a better understanding of the disabled people
   D. all of the above

4. Which one is the best definition for the underlined phrase "be exposed to" in Para. 4?

A. Learn something with.

B. Be given the chance to experience something new.

C. Able to accept different ideas and situation.

D. Take care of.

5. What is the greatest advantage of the intergenerational programs?

A. The old can take care of the young.

B. It will save the energy of the children's parents.

C. The children will learn a lot.

D. The old and the young will accompany each other.

Passage two

Children Can Still Detect Emotions Despite Face Masks[6]

NW: 332   GL: 12.2   AWL percentage: 5.53%   Keywords: children; emotions; face masks

Children have adorable ways of reacting to their environment. They are indeed very sensitive to their loved ones and pay close attention to their emotional states.

Now, a new study is revealing that children can still detect people's emotions even when they are wearing masks, reported PsyPost. "To slow the spread of the COVID-19, both the Centers for Disease Control[7] and the World Health Organization[8] have recommended wearing face coverings in public spaces," lead researcher Ashley Ruba, a postdoctoral researcher at the University of Wisconsin-Madison's Child Emotion Lab, told PsyPost. "This recommendation has led to speculation and concern by parents about the ramifications of mask wearing on emotion communication. We wanted to test if those concerns were well-founded.

The research involved showing 81 children aged 7 to 13 years old photos of faces that were sad, angry, or fearful, some were wearing a mask or sunglasses. The researchers did find that the children were more accurate in understanding emotions when faces were not covered but they performed almost as well when reading faces with sunglasses or face masks.

The children were found to spot the correct emotion of uncovered faces as often as 66% of the time while they correctly identified sadness about 28% of the time, anger 27% of the time, and fear 18% of the time in faces with masks. "Children can likely make reasonably accurate inferences about other people's emotions, even though people are often wearing masks. This should put parents' minds at ease about how mask-weaning might impact this aspect of child development," Ruba told PsyPost.

Still, the researcher has some practical advice to help parents and others when communicating with children during the pandemic.

"When you are trying to covey emotions to children (or anyone else) while wearing a mask, label how you are feeling, gesture, and use your voice. Children can use these cues to infer how you are feeling," Ruba said.

---

6   From INTERESTING ENGINEERING website.
7   Centers for Disease Control: 美国疾病控制中心
8   the World Health Organization: 世界卫生组织

1. What is the purpose of Ashley Ruba's research?

   A. To test whether children like to wear masks or not.

   B. To test whether masks have impact on children's health.

   C. To test whether the concerns about the impacts of mask on emotion are valid.

   D. To test whether there are disadvantages when children wear masks.

2. Which of the following is true from the passage?

   A. Children are afraid of wearing masks.

   B. Wearing masks has no influences on children's ability to understand emotions.

   C. Children have strong reaction to the emotion of angry.

   D. Children can't communicate with other people when they are wearing masks.

3. What's the meaning of "put…at ease" in Para.4?

   A. Reassure.

   B. Have an influence on.

   C. Worry about.

   D. Be happy with.

4. When you want to convey your feeling to children while wearing a mask, you should _____.

   A. use the gesture

   B. use the voice

   C. label your feeling

   D. all of the above

5. What can we infer from the passage?

   A. Wearing masks is good for people's health.

   B. Our emotion can be understood under the masks.

   C. Adults can't identify other people's emotions.

   D. The COVID-19 has a great impact on communication between children and parents.

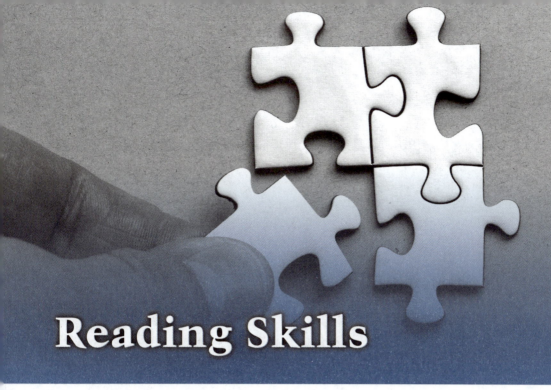

Reading Skills

Sequencing Information

When you sequence information, you put things in the order in which they occur. This can help you understand how key events in a text relate to each other, such as cause and effect relationships. It is especially useful to sequence information from stories or biographical texts. "Cause and effect" is regarded as a logical pattern commonly used in explanation and argumentation, especially when we explore possible connections between an action/event and its outcome, or between causes and results of an event, action, etc.

Exercises

Please read the above reading skill of sequencing information, and use it to give the story order in Short Passage One entitled "People of All Ages".

Sequencing order: _____

THINK

Academic Words in Use

Fill in the blanks in the following sentences with the appropriate words provided in the box below. Change the form of the words if necessary.

| depress | communicate | location | feature | mental | range |
| expose | expand | response | environment | community | benefit |

1. Being turned down by the girl he loved made Mike _____.
2. The writer's career _____ from these best-selling books.
3. As soon as men leave the aerosphere, they are _____ to the radiation.
4. There were 80 students whose ages _____ from 10 to 18.
5. You can _____ with anyone and send almost any documents and pictures over the Internet.
6. We meet once a month to discuss _____ problems.
7. The headmaster is drafting a plan for the _____ of our school.
8. I got a complete _____ block as soon as the interviewer asked me a question.
9. It is hard to find a suitable _____ for the desert scenes.
10. The _____ damage is caused by the chemical industry.
11. His question failed to get a(n) _____ from any of the students.
12. The house has many interesting _____, including a large Victorian fireplace.

Writing

For this part, you are allowed 30 minutes to read the following paragraphs and continue writing to make it a well-structured article. You should write at least 120 words but no more than 180 words.

Should Emotions Be Taught in Schools?

Who taught you how to identify and manage your emotions, how to recognize them when they arose and how to navigate your way through them? For may adults, the answer is: No one. You hacked your way through those confusing thickets on your own.

Recently, a number of researchers believe emotional skills should rank as high in importance in children's education as math, reading, history and science.

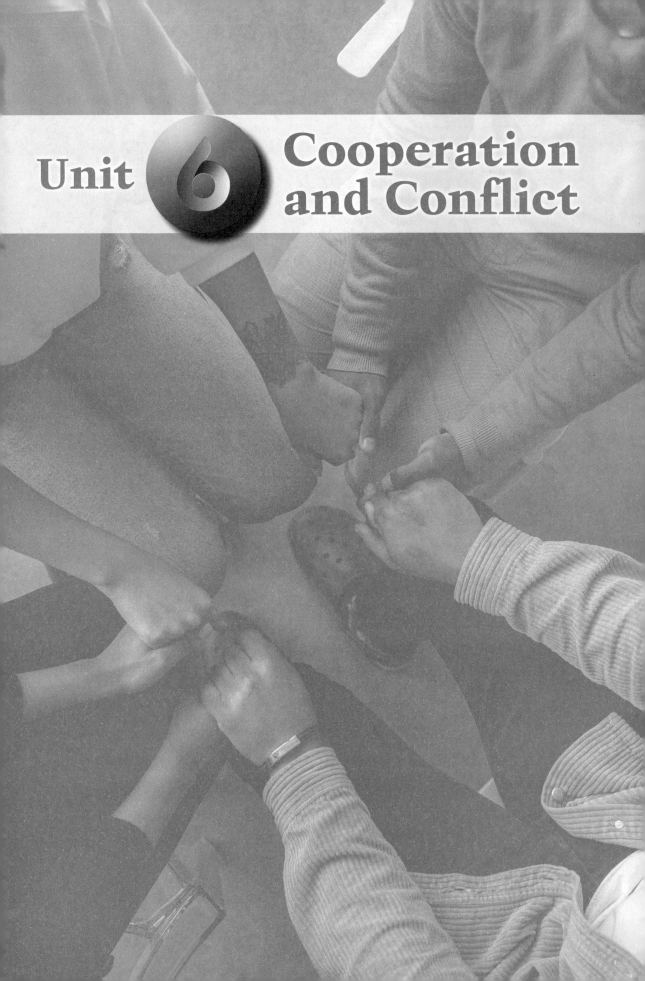

Unit 6 Cooperation and Conflict

Viewing

What Is a Cooperative?

About the video clip

This video clip discusses why cooperative is necessary, what is a cooperative and its benefits.

Understanding the video clip

Watch the video clip and fill in the blanks in the table below.

1. Why cooperative is necessary?	Being an owner in a business gives people _____ and a _____ in its success. But over the last thirty years, the number of people who _____ the businesses that _____ has become smaller. It's no surprise people say they have no influence: no influence _____, over the business and _____ as a whole. Cooperatives offer a solution.
2. What is a cooperative?	Cooperatives are owned in control together by the people _____: employees, customers, _____, suppliers, not _____. They have _____ in how the business is run and they even decide _____.

3. What are the benefits of cooperatives?	There are nearly 7,000 _____ co-ops in the UK. They're found in every sector, from _____ _____ to _____, cooperative pubs and _____ _____. Co-ops contribute 37 billion pounds each year to the British economy and boost UK _____. Cooperatives give all of us more control over _____ _____.

Further thoughts

Cooperative is a popular form to start a business. There are pros and cons of the cooperative that one needs to consider before deciding whether it is the right type of business. List some of them in the table below.

Pros of cooperative	Cons of cooperative
1. It can reduce business risks.	1. It has fewer incentives for large investors.
2. It can enable a large purchase in a group.	2. It is time-consuming for making decisions.
…	…

Banked Cloze

Below is a passage with ten blanks. You are required to select one word for each blank from the list of choices given in a word bank following the passage. Read the passage carefully before making your choices. Each choice in the blank is identified by a letter. Please write the corresponding letter for each item in the blanks. You may not use any of the words in the bank more than once.

Why Team Work Matters for Children[1]

NW: 234 **GL:** 8.9 **AWL percentage:** 6.06% **Keywords:** teamwork; children; social skill

"Getting along and engaging with others is the building block of many things in life," says clinical psychologist and parenting adviser Claire Halsey. "From a young age, children need to learn how to give and take, share, take turns, play to their strengths and 1._____ in other people to fill the gaps. It's a core 2._____ skill."

Ian Brember, founder of Big Hat Bushcamp, agrees. "It's a(n) 3._____ life skill for everyone, regardless of age," he says. "Whatever a child ends up doing as a job, they have to be able to work with other people. They also need to 4._____ relationships, whether with family members, friends, neighbors, colleagues or customers."

Learning to work as part of a team will help your child 5._____ many social

---

1 From The School Run website.

skills, such as patience, empathy, communication, respect for others, compromise and tolerance. It also helps them develop 6._____ in themselves and trust in other people.

The primary school years are 7._____ with opportunities for them to develop those skills. It is also an excellent time to 8._____ the teamwork ethos your child will draw on throughout their life, and many activities inside and outside the classroom can help children get used to being team players. And children who get to 9._____ with teamwork from a young age will act as 10. _____ role models for other kids, too.

A) learn	B) build	C) positive
D) grip	E) vital	F) draw
G) know	H) hone	I) connecting
J) power	K) social	L) packed
M) active	N) cultivate	O) confidence

Long Passage

You are going to read a passage with ten statements attached to it. Each statement contains information given in one of the paragraphs. Identify the paragraph from which the information is derived. You may choose a paragraph more than once. Each paragraph is marked with a letter. Please answer the questions by writing the corresponding letter after the statements.

Anything Is Possible when China and the United States Choose to Cooperate[2]

NW: 1,029 **GL:** 10.2 **AWL percentage:** 5.76%
Keywords: the United States; cooperation; China

A Good to see you all here. I would like to thank *China Daily* for providing us with this important opportunity for discussion. As the new year has begun, and a new US administration was just sworn in, it is particularly timely and meaningful for us to gather here to explore the future of China-US relations.

B Last year was extremely challenging. The world was hit by the unprecedented COVID-19 pandemic, and China-US relations suffered the worst setback of the last forty years. Despite all these, as a Chinese proverb says, "Every new year brings new

---

2 From CHINADAILY website.

beginnings and possibilities." I sincerely hope that the new year of 2021 will bring a new start to the world and to China-US relations.

C   This year marks the 50th anniversary of Dr. Kissinger's[3] historic visit to China as well as the famous "ping-pong diplomacy[4]". And as the story of "the tiny ball moved the big ball" goes, it took those great men before us extraordinary wisdom and courage to break the ice in China-US relations. The challenges we face today call for the same vision and courage to break the ice again.

D   President Joe Biden[5] has visited China a total of four times, and has a better knowledge of China. He first visited China as a young Senator in 1979 and met with Mr. Deng Xiaoping. It was the same year the two countries normalized bilateral relations. I read his inauguration speech[6] with great interest, and was especially impressed by his repeated appeal to the American people for unity over division. I believe we need exactly the same spirit for China-US relations.

E   In my interview with NBC[7] last year, I said the real enemy of the United States is COVID-19, not China. We are saddened by the loss of over 400,000 American lives to COVID-19, even more than the number of Americans lost in World War II. I cannot stop thinking about what could have been done differently. Had the Donald Trump[8] administration chosen science and cooperation over scapegoating and political games, how many lives could have been saved?

F   The Trump administration's misguided China policy in the past four years has proven an utter failure in meeting the common challenge like COVID-19. We should learn an important lesson from such failure. China and the United States, as two major countries in the world, should treat each other as partners rather than adversaries, help rather than fight each other, and, as the Americans like to say, "lead with the power of example rather than the example of power."

G   In his congratulatory message to then President-elect Joe Biden, President Xi Jinping stated that China and the United States should act "in the spirit of no conflict, no confrontation, mutual respect and win-win cooperation, so as to focus on cooperation, manage differences, move the relationship forward in a sound and steady manner and, together with other countries and the international community, advance the

---

3　Henry Alfred Kissinger: 美国著名外交官，在中美正常化的进程中发挥了重要作用。
4　ping-pong diplomacy: 乒乓外交，指 1971 年中国邀请美国乒乓球队访华事件。此举对中美关系的突破产生了影响，被誉为"小球推动大球"。
5　Joe Biden: 乔•拜登，美国第 46 任总统
6　inauguration speech: 就职演说
7　NBC (National Broadcasting Company): 美国全国广播公司
8　Donald Trump: 唐纳德•特朗普，美国第 45 任总统

noble cause of world peace and development." President Xi's vision is clear. The direction and path forward is also clear. Please allow me to explain this vision by quoting four "R" words.

H   The first R is "respect". Mutual respect is the foundation for successful people-to-people and state-to-state interactions. It is not a difficult starting point. China has stated repeatedly that it has no intention to challenge or replace the United States. We don't even think the relationship should be defined by "competition", because we keep challenging ourselves, not the United States. The only thing that China asks of the United States is to respect the development path we have chosen, respect our legitimate interests, and respect our pursuit for a better life, and to quit its obsession with changing or splitting China. The world would be better off if our two countries would respect and help each other succeed.

I   The second R is "reversal". The last four years' journey of our relationship has seen too many "traps" of mistrust, "pitfalls" of division and "poison" of hatred. Enough is enough. We must act without further delay to reverse the wrong course. A lot of repair has to be done. I agree with American friends' suggestion that both sides take small steps first to create conditions for improving the relationship. But we have to act now to bring China-US relations back on track.

J   The third R is "renewal". Yes, our two countries are different, but our shared interests and needs for cooperation far outweigh our differences. We believe COVID-19, economic recovery and climate change could be priority areas for cooperation for the near term. The Chinese people empathize with the American plight under COVID-19. We will continue to support the US COVID response, increase experience-sharing on diagnostics and treatment, and work more closely with the United States on the research, production and distribution of vaccines. We will also enhance macroeconomic policy coordination with the United States to help global economic recovery.

K   The fourth R is "responsibility". As the Chinese proverb goes, "A bigger boat is meant to carry more weight." Likewise, American people believe that "responsibilities gravitate to the person who can shoulder them." As two major countries in the world, China and the United States should shoulder important responsibilities for world peace and development. Our choice and action today will have far-reaching impact on the future of our world. Our two countries enjoyed successful cooperation in the past. History has taught us that working together, we could get great things done to the benefit of the two countries and the world. In other words, anything is possible when China and the United States choose to cooperate.

L   I want to conclude with a quote from Shakespeare: "It is not in the stars to hold our destiny but in ourselves." China and the United States can work together to avoid the so-called Thucydides Trap⁹. There is no predestined fate for the world. The future of China-US relations, and the future of the world, depend on what vision we embrace and what choice we make.

1. There are three priority areas for the United States and China to cooperate in the near future. ☐
2. China has already shared its experience in the treatment of COVID-19 with America. ☐
3. Joe Biden used to be the Senator of the United States and has visited China several times. ☐
4. Last year US-China relations encountered the biggest challenge of the last forty years. ☐
5. The United States and China used to have good cooperation in the past. ☐
6. If the Trump administration has adopted a different policy, many American lives would have been saved. ☐
7. American society is very divided at the moment. ☐
8. The United Stats and China normalized bilateral relations in 1979. ☐
9. Dr. Kissinger visited China in the year of 1971. ☐
10. About 400,000 Americans died in World War Ⅱ. ☐

---

9 Thucydides Trap: 修昔底德陷阱，美国政治学者格雷厄姆·艾利森创造的一个术语，用来描述当新兴强国威胁到现有强国的国际霸主地位时导致的一种明显的战争倾向。

Short Passages

There are two passages in this module. Each passage is followed by some questions or unfinished statements. For each of them there are four choices marked A, B, C, and D. You should decide on the best choice and mark the corresponding letter.

Passage one

How to Say I'm Sorry (and Really Mean It)[10]

NW: 340   **GL:** 12.5   **AWL percentage:** 4.0%   **Keywords:** apology; admission; contrition

There's more to saying sorry than just saying "sorry". In fact, a study led by researchers at Ohio State University found that effective apologies have six components: expressing regret, explaining what went wrong, acknowledging responsibility, declaring repentance, offering to repair the situation, and requesting forgiveness. "The more of those components that were included, the more likely the apology was seen as credible," says Roy Lewicki, lead author of the study. That may seem like a lot to remember, but Lewicki found that two sentiments were the most essential: admission (acknowledgment of your responsibility and the other person's feelings) and contrition (remorse and commitment to future change).

---

10 From *Reader's Digest* by Fields L.

Sincerity trumps timing

Did you screw up royally? A little cool-off time could help. "Sometimes an immediate apology is called for," says Antony Manstead, a professor of psychology at Cardiff University. "But if the other party is angry at your perceived wrongdoing, it may be more effective to wait because their anger may prevent them from being receptive to an apology."

Waiting can benefit you too. "The best time to apologize is when one feels ready to sincerely apologize," says Etienne Mullet, research director at the Institute of Advanced Studies in Paris.

Explain, don't excuse

"Because admitting to being wrong is painful and can make people worried that they're a bad person, they often water down their apology with excuses." says Roger Giner-Sorolla, a professor at the University of Kent. The worst sort of excuse? Finger pointing. "Examples include 'I certainly apologize if I offended anyone' and 'I'm very sorry, but in my defense, you started it,'" says Ryan Fehr, a professor at the University of Washington's Foster School of Business.

Let your body do the talking

Experts agree that face-to-face apologies beat phoned-in, e-mailed, or handwritten ones. "Facial expressions, posture, and the tone of voice have all been shown to be important channels that convey sincerity when you express remorse," Giner-Sorolla says. "Anyone can type 'I feel really ashamed,' but if you say it live, it's obvious whether or not you mean it."

1. What does the underlined word "trumps" (Line 1, Para. 2) mean?
   A. Beats.
   B. Equals.
   C. Connects.
   D. Credits.

2. What should the most effective apologies be like?
   A. Just saying sorry.
   B. Asking for forgiveness.
   C. Explaining the reasons behind the action.
   D. Admitting your responsibility and expressing regret.

3. When is the best time to apologize?

   A. As soon as possible.

   B. When the other party is angry.

   C. When you are angry.

   D. When both you and the other party have cooled down and you feel ready to do.

4. Why do people like to find excuses when they apologize?

   A. Because people like to finger pointing.

   B. Because apologizing can make people feel offended.

   C. Because acknowledging one's wrong can make people feel unhappy and anxious.

   D. Because finding an excuse can make the other party happy.

5. What is the best form to make an apology?

   A. Making a phone call.

   B. Apologizing face-to-face.

   C. Writing a letter.

   D. Writing an e-mail.

Passage two

The International Day of Friendship[11]

NW: 369　GL: 9.9　AWL percentage: 2.7%　Keywords: international; friendship; celebration

Friends come in all shapes and sizes. They may be someone we met as a child, a classmate at school, someone we met at work or through other friends. They may be friends who live at a distance in another country or virtual friends we've made online. Whoever they are, however we met them, there is a special connection based on a shared history and interests, enjoying doing things together or simply talking and understanding each other. Friends are there to help us at difficult times and to celebrate the good times. Doctors say that friends are very important for both our physical and mental health at all stages in life.

But friends are not only important on an individual level. Friendship can also be important on a global level. Friendships that cross borders can help bring peace and avoid war. Learning to think of other people, people who are different from us, as our friends help us work together to build a culture of peace. That's why the UN declared 30 July as its official International Day of Friendship.

An international celebration was first suggested by the World Friendship Crusade[12]. This organization was founded by Dr Ramón Artemio Bracho and his friends in Puerto Pinasco, Paraguay, in 1958. They wanted to support the power of friendship and its importance in creating a culture of peace. So, in the same year, they decided to celebrate Friendship Week in Puerto Pinasco and other places in Paraguay. The following year, they repeated the week and finished on 30 July, which they declared as Friendship Day. From there, celebrations of friendship grew and spread across the Americas, then the world, and eventually the UN declared an International Day of Friendship in 2011.

The International Day of Friendship on 30 July is not the only day celebrating friendship around the world. A number of countries, such as Paraguay, also celebrate on 30 July, but other countries have different dates. For example, Argentina, Brazil and Spain celebrate Friend's Day on 20 July, while in India and the US, they celebrate it on the first Sunday in August. In Finland and Estonia, Friendship Day is celebrated on the same day as Valentine's Day, 14 February.

11　From United Nations website.
12　**World Friendship Crusade**: 世界友谊运动是一个国际民间组织，由 Ramón Artemio Bracho 博士于 1958 年在巴拉圭的皮纳斯科港创立，旨在倡导友谊，促进和平文化。

1. What does the underlined word "virtual" (Line 3, Para. 1) mean?

   A. Sincere.

   B. True.

   C. Almost actual.

   D. Close.

2. What can be learned from Paragraph one?

   A. Anyone can become our friend.

   B. Our childhood pal can no longer become friend in adulthood.

   C. It is easy to make friends with people from a another country.

   D. Someone who becomes our friend usually has a special connection with us.

3. According to the passage, why did UN declare its official International Day of Friendship?

   A. Because people all over the world wanted an International Day of Friendship.

   B. Because it is very important for both people's physical and mental health.

   C. Because friendships among different nations can bring peace.

   D. Because it is a popular celebration worldwide.

4. When was Friendship Day first celebrated?

   A. 1958.

   B. 1959.

   C. 1960.

   D. 2011.

5. When is the International Day of Friendship celebrated in the US?

   A. 14th of February.

   B. 30th of July.

   C. 20th of July.

   D. The first Sunday in August.

Reading Skills

Facts and Opinions

A writer may give both facts and opinions in his/her writing. Facts are statements that tell what has really happened or really is the case. Opinions are statements of personal belief, judgement or feeling about a subject.

Read the following statements by someone talking about the advantages of an electronic ticketing system:

The advantages are perhaps obvious for using one smart-card for many transportation systems. In Hong Kong, the Octopus has already enabled operators, especially the MTR, to successfully process more passengers (2.5 million a day) with greater speed and efficiency than any other previous system.

In the above statements, the writer first speaks cautiously about the advantages of the smart-card. Note that the writes uses the word "perhaps" to show his opinion. Then the writer presents a statement of fact: What the smart-card Octopus has done in Hong Kong.

Sometimes, facts and opinions may be mixed together, making it hard for the reader to dissociate one from the other. Consequently, readers shall be always alert to the opinion clue words that appear in the passage.

The following are types of opinion clue words:

1. Some words state an opinion by evaluating or making a judgement: stupid, clever, kind, evil, well dressed or sloppy.

2. Some words clearly show that an opinion will follow, such as: I believe, I think, in my opinion.

3. Some words indicate that there may be some doubt in a statement, such as: sometimes, possible, probably, likely, perhaps, on occasion, maybe.

Exercises

Write F before each statement of fact below; write O before each statement of opinion.

1. Giant's marketing efforts are prodigious.

2. It is spending half of its $12 million annual advertising budget this year on sponsorships of professional racing teams.

3. Giant started out in the rice paddies of Taichung 26 years ago, producing bikes sold under other companies' brand names in 1980.

4. Within a decade, the company had carved a niche for itself in the mountain bike market.

5. The weather doesn't look very promising.

THINK

Academic Words in Use

Fill in the blanks in the following sentences with the appropriate words provided in the box below. Change the form of the words if necessary.

solution	available	privilege	significant	immense	expect
fulfill	overwhelmingly	tackling	minimum	capture	instill

1. Under _____ pressure of epidemic prevention and control at home, China has offered urgently-needed supplies to others within its capacity.
2. China has made remarkable contributions to global causes aimed at _____ climate change.
3. Teams have basic needs that must be _____ if you expect your teams to experience their greatest success.
4. Creativity, innovation, and different viewpoints are _____ and encouraged.
5. Ever since I was very young, my parents _____ in me the value of writing thank-you notes.
6. In fact, your brain is the fattiest organ in your body, consisting of a(n) _____ of 60 percent fat.
7. Familiarity and experience are the long term _____ to the problem of culture shock.
8. I also carry around a notebook in my purse to _____ the thoughts I'm coming up with.
9. This will mean that more jobs will be _____ for more people.
10. Leadership is the most _____ word in today's competitive business environment.
11. No longer is the possession of information confined to a(n) _____ minority.
12. Employment remains the _____ important form of work and source of income for most people.

Writing

For this part, you are allowed 30 minutes to read the following paragraphs and continue writing to make it a well-structured article. You should write at least 120 words but no more than 180 words.

Competition or Cooperation, a Dilemma?

Today, many people believe that it is vital to cultivate the spirit of competitiveness in early childhood education. Parents always say that life is a constant battle and one has to be competitive to emerge out of it successfully. However, some argue that competition could also lead to negative outcomes, thus cooperation and teamwork spirit should be encouraged instead.

In my view, the two views should not be contradictory, and it is important for us to examine both sides to reach a sound conclusion.

Unit 7 Entrepreneurship

Viewing

How to Be an Entrepreneur?

About the video clip

This video clip discusses how to become an entrepreneur.

Understanding the Video Clip

Watch the video clip and fill in the blanks in the table below.

How do you get to be an entrepreneur? Most of the advice focuses on 1._____.
At the heart of successful entrepreneurship lies something oddly more abstract and 2._____ into the causes of human unhappiness.
The bigger and more 3._____ what you're trying to fix happens to be, the more successful your business can be, because 4._____ is now well developed.
One could go on and on. Our griefs and 5._____ are endless.
However difficult the journey, your business will 6._____ making money and benefit in humanity, too.

Further thoughts

The video clip talks about both the traditional view on starting up a business and the entrepreneurship opportunities. List what you catch from the viewing.

Advice of starting up a business	Something that may frustrate and depress us (Entrepreneurship opportunities)
1. writing a business plan	1. getting on with one's partner
2. raising money	2. educating children
...	...

Banked Cloze

Below is a passage with ten blanks. You are required to select one word for each blank from the list of choices given in a word bank following the passage. Read the passage carefully before making your choices. Each choice in the blank is identified by a letter. Please write the corresponding letter for each item in the blanks. You may not use any of the words in the bank more than once.

Li Ziqi: A Blogger and Food Entrepreneur with One Foot in the Past and One Foot in the Future[1]

NW: 264 **GL:** 12.0 **AWL percentage:** 3.96% **Keywords:** sponsorship; launch; pursuit

Li Ziqi's video blogging career began in 2016, when she 1._____ with a video of herself baking rice inside a hollowed-out bamboo stalk. In an interview with Baidu's news vertical, Li said that she was looking for ways to make money in her small village. Li had left her village at the age of 14 to work in the city, where she cycled through gigs in 2._____ and DJ-ing[2], but moved back to her village after she felt too homesick to stay 3._____. Back home, she opened her own shop on Taobao, the Chinese internet retail 4._____, where she bought goods wholesale and re-sold them for higher. To drum up interest, she began experimenting with videos to promote her shop 5._____.

---

1 From Nü Women website.
2 DJ-ing: 做音乐节目主持人

There is another 6._____ of Li's brand easily missed by her international fans: her source of income. Li never mentions any endorsements or 7._____, because she already works for one brand—Li Ziqi herself. In June 2018, she returned to her initial reason for making videos. But instead of buying and re-selling other people's wholesale goods, Li 8._____ a line of "Li Ziqi" branded food and beverage products on Taobao.

Her 9._____, found on her official Weibo page, would suggest that she has already got everything that money can buy: "Working at sunrise, resting at sunset. Pure and 10._____ foods and a quiet lifestyle are the pursuit of my life."

A) presented	B) waitressing	C) progress
D) wholesale	E) slogan	F) resources
G) away	H) natural	I) element
J) platform	K) launched	L) debuted
M) innovatively	N) sponsorships	O) kick

Long Passage

You are going to read a passage with ten statements attached to it. Each statement contains information given in one of the paragraphs. Identify the paragraph from which the information is derived. You may choose a paragraph more than once. Each paragraph is marked with a letter. Please answer the questions by writing the corresponding letter after the statements.

A Work-Life Adventure[3]

NW: 994　**GL:** 9.7　**AWL percentage:** 5.1%　**Keywords:** envision; digital nomad; inspiration

A　　Nomads have been roaming the earth for centuries, living off the land but never having a permanent home. One can easily envision the Mongolian tribes surviving the cold winters in their yurts, or the Bedouins[4] herding sheep or goats across the Arabian Peninsula.[5]

B　　The word nomad is derived from the Greek word "nomas", meaning one who wanders in search of pasture. There are three types of nomads that are well-documented in history. First are the hunter-gatherers, who moved from place to place as different seasons yielded different animals, vegetables and fruit to subsist on. Second are the

---

[3] From *English Language Learning* by Bragg J.
[4] the Bedouins: 贝多因人
[5] the Arabian Peninsula: 阿拉伯半岛

pastoralists who travel around seeking pastures for their livestock. Finally, there are the peripatetic nomads who use their specialized skills to travel and work wherever they go. All three still exist today, but since the onset of industrialization, the latter is the most common.

C   However, there is a fourth type of nomad that has emerged in the last decade: the digital nomad. This is a person who is free to travel and live wherever he desires, given there are two things available: a computer and a decent Internet connection.

D   Digital nomads are people who don't want the typical 9-to-5 work life. Through the use of technology, they instead opt for a lifestyle that allows for a schedule and the freedom to choose their own workload and working hours. And while they are accountable to whoever hires them, they can avoid the daily doldrums of the office.

E   The number of digital nomads in the world is hard to count, but this trend is on the rise. If you were to travel to Southeast Asia, for example, to a country like Thailand, chances are you will see digital nomad. It could be someone working on their computer in a local coffee shop or restaurant or lying on the beach under an umbrella with a laptop and a cool drink.

F   "Workers are becoming more confident in their employment options," says Sara Sutton Fell, the founder and CEO of FlexJobs[6], a website that posts job listings to those seeking flexible, often remote, work arrangements. She adds: "People are ready to take advantage of a stronger job market to find a flexible job that better suits their lives."

G   As more people are looking beyond the conventional office jobs in favor of something more adventurous, there has been an explosion in websites and articles that offer advice for the would-be wanderer. From travel and living tips to practical financial and logistical advice, one needs not go far to find inspiration and ideas.

H   Here are some examples of advice that is offered:

1. Do your research on the place you plan to go to. What is the cost of living? How much does a meal cost at a mid-scale restaurant? Are there organizations that introduce people to each other?

2. Learn how to live with one suitcase (maybe two). This will make it much easier to move around and reduce the costs and muscle strain of moving bags around from one place to the next.

3. Be open-minded and treat your destination as your new home. Meet people,

---

6 FlexJobs: 一家介绍灵活性工作的中介公司

explore the city, and have fun!

4. Get travel health insurance. You never know when something can happen. So better to be safe than stuck with a massive medical bill.

I   A good go-to resource for digital nomads is Nomadlist.com. It boasts a large, crowd-sourced database of cities, arranged in thumbnail snapshots on its homepage. "These thumbnails offer details of the average Internet speed, cost of living per month, and temperature for any given place. For example, in Chiang Mai, Thailand, the average cost of living is 907 U.S. dollars per month, the Internet speed is 20 megabits per second and the temperature is a nice 24 degrees in winter. Jeju Island in the Republic of Korea costs 1,560 U.S. dollars per month, the Internet is a speedy 99 megabits per second, and the temperature is a cooler 10 degrees.

J   While this may sound like a dream life, the reality can be much different. Working remotely can be isolating and lonely. A person can become easily distracted and adopt poor habits. Luckily, there has been another trend on the rise that can directly tackle this problem. It's called coworking. Coworking spaces are offices in which people who work independently come together and share a place to work. Usually the space has all the accoutrements of a typical office: desks, chairs, tables, printers, good Internet connection, coffee and snacks. Workers can pay a monthly fee to have unlimited access to the space, and spaces can range from the very basic office setup to a lavish, modern facility with comfortable soft chairs, sofas and cool tables.

K   *The Harvard Business Review*[7] published an article at the end of 2017 about how beneficial coworking spaces can be. It found that the majority of people surveyed who work in these spaces say they are less lonely (83%) and happier since they joined (89%). But the concept of a coworking space is not simply for the advantage of work efficiency. The social aspect of coworking spaces is vital to many people who use them. Members can motivate each other and inspire new ideas, share business contacts and network. The concept has proven to be very successful. It is estimated that by 2020, the number of coworking space members worldwide will at least double.

L   The nomadic life isn't for everyone. It does involve some risk-taking and flexibility, and not everyone can handle the feeling of being in a place temporarily or living out of a suitcase. However, it does offer something different from the daily grind of life back home and has given countless people the freedom they would not have had before the age of technology.

---

7 *The Harvard Business Review*:《哈佛商业评论》是1922年哈佛大学商学院创办的杂志，致力于给全世界的专业人士提供缜密的管理见解和最好的管理实践。

1. There is a website which can offer very specific information database of cities, costs, local temperature and so on. ☐
2. Coworking space can promote work efficiency, business contacts and inspire new ideas. ☐
3. The drawbacks of working remotely and the solution to this working style. ☐
4. Enormous websites and articles provide a variety of advice for the potential wanderers. ☐
5. The number of digital nomads are on the rise globally. ☐
6. The founder of a website that posts job listings is optimistic about flexible working options of time and space. ☐
7. The forth type of nomad is the digital nomad with a computer and a decent Internet connection. ☐
8. Three types of well-documented nomads still exist today. ☐
9. The number of coworking space members worldwide will increase twice by 2020. ☐
10. Digital nomads have the freedom to choose their own workload and working hours. ☐

Short Passages

There are two passages in this module. Each passage is followed by some questions or unfinished statements. For each of them there are four choices marked A, B, C, and D. You should decide on the best choice and mark the corresponding letter.

Passage one

Meet the Entrepreneur Turning Your Footsteps into Energy[8]

NW: 333 **GL:** 9.1 **AWL percentage:** 4.51% **Keywords:** energy; radiate; innovation

Could turning our footsteps into electricity help meet our energy needs? One young eco-entrepreneur[9] thinks so.

Laurence Kemball Cook seems like the kind of young man any mother would want her daughter to bring home. He has a neat, healthy, clean-cut appearance and a polite, even charming manner. His office near London's King's Cross Station is relaxed, a little scruffy, filled with informally dressed staff who all radiate the same air of youthful enthusiasm as

---

8 From Reader's digest website.
9 eco-entrepreneur: 环保行业创业者

their boss.

Yet this 30-year-old engineer, inventor, and entrepreneur is by his own admission an obsessive workaholic. "Some people would probably say that I'm a perfectionist, to a point that can be quite frustrating," he says.

Laurence admits, "The idea of generating energy from footsteps isn't new and other people have tried it. They're using things such as the piezo-electric crystals you find in cigarette lighters to create a charge. But the power is so low that you can never do anything meaningful with that energy." Laurence took a completely different route. The weight of a footstep on his tile makes a horizontal flywheel inside it rotate.

"The more people walk, the more this flywheel spins," he explains. "Then we withdraw the power from the flywheel as we need it. We can suck it out bit by bit." Every pedestrian that passes over a tile generates around seven watts in energy. Moreover, Laurence's ambitions are as much moral as commercial. Once the tiles are manufactured, the system requires no fossil fuels, generates no CO_2 and produces no pollutants, which is why he says, "Some people might define their aims as wealth or success, but for me it's just, Let's get it out there and do good."

But could this really make a difference to everyday energy use? Julie Hirigoyen, chief executive of Britain's branch of the non-profit World Green Building Council, thinks so. Pavegen[10] is a "hugely innovative technology", she says. She likes the way that it "engages users and makes them aware that they're helping to solve a problem. We certainly need every clever form of renewable solution."

1. **What does the underlined word "workaholic" (Line 2, Para. 3) refer to?**

   A. A person who likes to drink alcohol.
   B. A person who feels the compulsive need to work.
   C. A person who would like to work under stress.
   D. A person who doesn't want to work.

2. **What is the main idea of Paragraph 4?**

   A. Laurence is the first person who has the idea of generating energy from footsteps.
   B. People have tried piezo-electric crystals to create a charge.

---

10 Pavegen: 环保踩踏地砖

C. Laurence takes a step at using people's weight of footsteps to generate energy.

D. Generating clean energy is still the challenge of the whole world.

3. **What is Laurence's attitude toward energy-oriented business entrepreneurship?**

A. The business should be profitable.

B. Entrepreneurs should only think about profit.

C. Entrepreneurs should take both morals and business into consideration.

D. The business values do nothing with morals of society.

4. **What is the distinctive characteristic of Laurence's Pavegen?**

A. Innovative.

B. Cheap.

C. Eco-friendly.

D. Profitable.

5. **What can we conclude from Laurence's entrepreneurship?**

A. Ambitious.

B. Responsible.

C. Creative.

D. Novel.

Passage two

The Man Who Sells Everything[11]

NW: 448   **GL:** 10.5   **AWL percentage:** 6.08%   **Keywords:** entrepreneur; contemplate; breed

US entrepreneur Jeff Bezos[12] has built Amazon[13] from a small online bookseller into a retail giant. After graduating from Princeton University in 1986 with a degree in electrical engineering and computer science, Jeff Bezos went to work on Wall Street. In 1994, he quit finance to try his hand as an entrepreneur. Amazon.com started as an online bookseller, selling its first copies in July 1995. In the years since, it has grown into a diversified retail giant, as well as a producer of consumer electronics, such as the Kindle[14], and a major provider of cloud-computing services. When asked whether Bezos realized that Amazon would become the <u>behemoth</u>, Bezos said: "There were indications that we were on to something from the very beginning. The original business plan contemplated only books and growing a relatively small company. But shortly after launching, we had already sold books in all 50 US states and 45 countries. A couple of years after that, we sent an email message to about 1,000 customers and asked, "Besides the things we sell today, what would you like to see us sell?" The answers came back so long-tailed (distant to the core business)—people said, "Windshield wiper blades for my car, and so on. At that point we started to realize that perhaps we could sell a very wide selection of things using the methods that we had pioneered."

When talked about the crucial qualities that make for a successful entrepreneur, one is that view of divine discontent: How can you make something better? Entrepreneurship and invention are pretty closely coupled. Inventors are always thinking, "I'm kind of inured to this, but just because I'm used to it doesn't mean it can't be improved." Entrepreneurs also benefit greatly from being willing to fail, willing to experiment. Good entrepreneurs tend to be stubborn on the vision but flexible on the details. People wonder what are the keys to running a large business in an entrepreneurial way? Bezos stated: "A pioneering culture that rewards experimentation even as it embraces the fact that it is going to lead to failure—that is very important for larger companies. And a long-term orientation is a key part of that. Some argue that Amazon does well by its customers but not so well for small businesses. We are very empowering to certain small businesses. We have millions of small sellers who get access to our prime retail real estate and sell right alongside us. The great

---

11   From Reader's Digest ASIA website.
12   Jeff Bezos: 亚马逊购物网创始人兼总裁
13   Amazon: 亚马逊购物网
14   Kindle: 由亚马逊设计和销售的电子阅读器

thing about ideas is that every new idea leads to two more. It's the opposite of a gold rush[15] where the more people who show up, the faster the gold runs out. Ideas are not like that; ideas breed."

1. What does the underlined **behemoth** (Line 8, Paragraph 1) mean?

   A. A bookstore.

   B. A retail giant.

   C. A small grocery store.

   D. A building.

2. When did Bezos start to sell everything at Amazon.com?

   A. From the very beginning of start-up of Amazon.com.

   B. After receiving a long list of responses from the selling-item survey of 1,000 customers.

   C. In 1995.

   D. After selling books in all 50 US states and 45 countries.

3. According to Bezos, what is the vital quality of making for a successful entrepreneur?

   A. Being diligent and hard-working.

   B. Being clever and tactful.

   C. Divine discontent.

   D. Focusing on details.

4. What is the passage mainly talking about?

   A. Bezos had a clear goal of founding a huge online supermarket from the very beginning.

   B. Amazon.com sold everything when it was founded.

   C. Bezos respected his customers' opinions and was willing to pioneer in some uncertain field.

   D. Entrepreneurs should be very diligent and hard-working.

---

15 gold rush: 淘金热

5. **Which statement is true according to the passage?**

   A. Bezos majored in finance and computer science.
   B. Amazon sold books and other goods from the very beginning of its start-up.
   C. Bezos believes that business ideas are not like gold rush.
   D. Great entrepreneurs are stubborn on details while flexible on visions.

Reading Skills

Reading Longer Passages Effectively

Like a paragraph, a longer passage focuses on a single topic, expresses a general idea about that topic, follows a pattern of organization, and uses signal words and phrases to indicate supporting ideas.

1 The topic

The topic of a longer passage is usually repeated many times to focus the reader's attention and to reinforce connections between the topic and the supporting ideas. It is generally mentioned in:

- the title;

- the topic sentence of each paragraph;

- at least one other sentence in each paragraph.

2 The thesis statement

In a longer passage, the writer's idea about the topic is stated in a sentence called the thesis statement. Like the main idea in a paragraph, the thesis statement tells the writer's overall idea about the topic. Recognizing and understanding the writer's thesis statement is the key to understanding the ideas in a passage.

3 Identifying the thesis statement

The thesis statement in English

• includes the topic;

• is usually found in the first paragraph (or paragraphs);

• is always a complete sentence;

• often indicates how the ideas will be developed in the passage;

• is supported by the ideas and information found in all of the paragraphs of the passage.

In English, the thesis statement is near the beginning of a passage because readers expect to learn right away what the passage is about. In other languages and cultures, this is not necessarily true.

Think about how writers express their ideas in your language. Where can you usually find the thesis in a longer passage in your language? Is it the same as in English or different?

Exercises

Please read the above reading skill of reading longer passages effectively and use the guidelines to find out the thesis statement in Short Passage Two entitled "The Man Who Sells Everything".

The thesis statement: _____

_____

_____

THINK

Academic Words in Use

Fill in the blanks in the following sentences with the appropriate words provided in the box below. Change the form of the words if necessary.

| capture | male | launch | industrial | virtual | fascinate |
| affection | annoy | normal | emission | emphasize | assign |

1. If you find yourself getting impatient or _____ with people over unimportant things, you'd better control your stress.

2. I was _____ to work at an office near my mother's house, so I stayed with her for a month.

3. Over the years, designers and artists have been trying to _____ the essentials of good design.

4. Another trend is off-site or _____ management, where teams of people linked by email and the Internet work on projects from their own houses.

5. Some experts say that women will become more effective managers than men because they have the power to reach common goals in a way traditional _____ managers cannot.

6. The poem revealed a parent's _____ when her child grows up and leaves.

7. Gas _____ have been effectively reduced in developed countries.

8. A new marketing policy will be _____ on June 18th.

9. Escalators at the station _____ carried 2,500 people between 8:30 am and 9:30 am on a typical day.

10. The current education system excessively _____ the value of academic performance.

11. I was now _____ by the idea and words of the poetry.

12. Temperatures have risen since the _____ age began in the 19th century.

Writing

For this part, you are allowed 30 minutes to read the following paragraphs and continue writing to make it a well-structured article. You should write at least 120 words but no more than 180 words.

My View on Entrepreneurship

Due to the increasing number of college graduates, it is difficult for students to find a job because of the fierce competition. Traditional jobs are fully employed. The government encourages graduates to start their own businesses.

I think entrepreneurship encouragement is a good policy. On the one hand, graduates can give full play to their talents. They can choose to do what they are good at, instead of carrying out plans and executing them in the office. Compared with command, self-employment is more creative.

Unit 8 Career Development

Viewing

Apple CEO Tim Cook Talking About Career Planning

About the video clip

This video clip discusses Apple CEO Tim Cook's thoughts on career plan.

Understanding the video clip

Please watch the video clip and fill in the blanks in the table below.

1. Normally I would never remember this, but I was doing a _____ a few years ago.
2. Maybe you have much more _____ into what you may be doing, but for me the journey was not predictable at all.
3. It goes sort of back to the Lincoln quote… the only thing I believe you can do is (to) _____.
4. The companies that you work for are going to _____.
5. Stay with _____ and let those things go on about you.

Further thoughts

Watch the video clip again, and discuss with your partner on the question "Have you found your north star?". If not yet, what will you do to start your career planning? Write down your future plans and exchange ideas with your partner.

Banked Cloze

Below is a passage with ten blanks. You are required to select one word for each blank from the list of choices given in a word bank following the passage. Read the passage carefully before making your choices. Each choice in the blank is identified by a letter. Please write the corresponding letter for each item in the blanks. You may not use any of the words in the bank more than once.

Job Outlook Brightening for China Graduates[1]

NW: 296   **GL:** 12.0   **AWL percentage:** 8.25%   **Keywords:** job outlook; ranking; employability

Graduates of universities on the Chinese mainland have been enjoying a rise in their job 1._____ over the past decade, with it now listed as the fifth-most 2._____ country or region in a higher education report. The *Times Higher Education*[2] magazine and French consultancy Emerging[3] on Thursday released the Employability Rankings 2020, a 10-year survey into the places that provide the best opportunities for graduating students around the world.

The Chinese mainland's score increased by 132 percent, from 208 in 2010 to 481 this year, meaning the nation jumped from 11th place in the ranking of best-performing

---

1　From CHINADAILY Global Edition website.
2　*Times Higher Education*: 一本以高等教育咨询和发展为主要内容的英国杂志
3　Emerging: 一家法国咨询服务网站

countries and regions for 3._____. Universities in all countries and regions are rated, and the higher the university is in the rankings, the more points it achieves for its host nation. The study found that all Chinese mainland institutions either improved or 4._____ their previous rankings. One of the nation's top performers was the University of Science and Technology of China, which climbed seven places to 99th.

The country's overall performance in the latest rankings echoes its progress shown in the Times Higher Education World University Rankings 2021, which saw the research quality of its middle-ranking universities begin to 5._____ with those of the United States for the first time. The podium for this year's ranking is dominated by the most prestigious US institutions, with California Institute of Technology, the Massachusetts Institute of Technology and Harvard University 6._____ up the top three.

Jamie Ramacciotti, head of student content at the *Times Higher Education*, said: "Employability 7._____ the return of investment on education for many students and their families. The latest Employability Rankings show that students have a wide 8._____ of choice when it comes to study destinations that will help power the early years of their career." Students and parents are considering employability more 9._____ when it comes to deciding 10._____ to study.

A) making	B) challenges	C) where
D) represents	E) seriously	F) range
G) increased	H) converge	I) maintained
J) overall	K) prospects	L) competitive
M) employability	N) what	O) found

Long Passage

You are going to read a passage with ten statements attached to it. Each statement contains information given in one of the paragraphs. Identify the paragraph from which the information is derived. You may choose a paragraph more than once. Each paragraph is marked with a letter. Please answer the questions by writing the corresponding letter after the statements.

Should You Go to a Graduate School?[4]

NW: 797 **GL:** 12.3 **AWL percentage:** 6.29% **Keywords:** potential; reinvent; pioneer

A   Although the rich world is enjoying a long spell of unprecedented job growth and low unemployment, competition for the most competitive roles remains fierce. Tech companies like Google and Microsoft reportedly receive two million applications per year, and banks like Goldman Sachs attract in the thousands.

B   While these employers, among a growing number of others, are unanimously highlighting the importance of critical soft skills—such as emotional intelligence, resilience, and learnability—as determinants of performance, the most in-demand jobs require graduate credentials, to the point of surpassing current levels of supply. Consider, for example, that there are around 500,000 open IT jobs, but only 50,000 new IT

---

4 From Harvard Business Review website.

graduates each year.

C   At the same time, the number of people enrolling in university continues to rise, effectively devaluating the undergraduate degree. In America, one-third of adults are college graduates, a figure that was just 4.6% in the 1940s. Globally, UNESCO reports that the number of students earning a university degree has more than doubled in the past 20 years.

D   In light of these figures, it is easy to understand why more and more of the workforce is considering going to graduate school. In the U.S., the number of graduate students has tripled since the 1970s, and according to some estimates, 27% of employers now require master's degrees for roles in which historically undergraduate degrees sufficed.

E   What, then, are the motives you should be considering if you are trying to decide whether or not to enroll? How can you determine if the time—and especially the money—required to pursue a graduate education will actually pay off or not? Here are some factors to consider: First of all, it's no secret that people who have graduate school degrees are generally paid more money than those who don't. While a 25% increase in earnings is the average boost people see, attending the top MBA programs can increase your salary by as much as 60%-150% (whereas a master's in Human Services or Museum Sciences will increase your earnings by a mere 10%-15%).

F   Moreover, AI[5] and automation are replacing many roles with others and a growing proportion of workers are being pushed to reskill and upskill to remain relevant. There's no doubt that most of us will have to reinvent ourselves at some point if we want to do the same. If you find yourself in this situation currently, grad school may not be a bad choice. The bigger challenge, however, will be picking what to major in. If you set yourself up to be a strong candidate for jobs that are in high demand, you risk being too late to the game by the time you graduate. For instance, if everyone studies data science in order to fill unfilled vacancies, in a few years there will be a surplus of candidates. A better strategy is do your research and try to predict what the in-demand roles will be in the future. Universities can actually help you here. Increasingly, formal study qualifications are being indexed according to the foundational, or soft skills, they require. This means that more graduate programs are starting to teach soft skills, in addition to knowledge, and prepare students for an uncertain labor market rather than for specific jobs.

G   It's not uncommon for people to get stuck in the wrong job as a result of poor career guidance or a lack of self-awareness at a young age—i.e. failing to know their interests and potential when they began their careers. This leads to low levels of engagement, performance, and productivity, and high levels of burnout, stress, and alienation.

---

5   AI: Artificial Intelligence（人工智能）的缩写

Pursuing your passion, therefore, is not a bad criterion for deciding to go to grad school. After all, people perform better and learn more when their studies align with their values. If you can nurture your curiosity and interests by pursuing rigorous learning, your expertise will be more likely to set you apart from other candidates, and increase the chances of ending up in a job you love.

H It seems, then, that the decision to go or not to go to grad school is as complex as uncertain, for there are no clear-cut arguments in favor of it or against it. To be sure, it is not easy to predict what the ROI (Return On Investment) of grad school will be, though the factors outlined here may help you assess your own individual circumstances. Like any big decision in life, this one requires a fair amount of courage and risk taking. In the words of Daniel Kahneman[6] the Nobel Prize-winning psychologist who pioneered the modern study of decision making under uncertainty: "Courage is willingness to take the risk once you know the odds. Optimistic overconfidence means you are taking the risk because you don't know the odds. It's a big difference."

1. Graduate education enables you to have the chance to correct your previous inappropriate direction of career.
2. It is your own individual circumstances to decide whether you should go to a grad school or not.
3. Graduate school education will increase your competition superiority to the development of AI and automation.
4. Graduate programs prepare you for more soft skills besides specific knowledge.
5. Decision making always demands courage and risk-taking.
6. Students with college experiences are on the dramatic rise around the globe.
7. A quarter of employers who just demand bachelors' degree request master's degree currently.
8. The competition of ideal employment remains fierce despite of a long period of optimistic situation.
9. Employers still emphasize graduate diplomas even in most of urgently-demanded job vacancies.
10. The critical motive of considering attending a graduate school is the income factor.

---

6 Daniel Kahneman: 丹尼尔·卡尼曼教授，2002年诺贝尔经济学奖得主，他因将"经济学和心理学研究有机结合，特别是有关在不确定状况下的决策制定的研究"而得奖。

Short Passages

There are two passages in this module. Each passage is followed by some questions or unfinished statements. For each of them there are four choices marked A, B, C, and D. You should decide on the best choice and mark the corresponding letter.

Passage one

What Should Every College Student Be Doing for Career Success?[7]

NW: 397 **GL:** 12.7 **AWL percentage:** 5.91% **Keywords:** career; internship; proactive

There are different types of college students: the ones who spend their years locked away in the library, the ones who leave everything to the last minute, the ones who spend more time socializing than studying, the ones who split their time between work and the classroom, the ones who do either one of the above things and the ones who try to do them all.

With all these experiences college comes with, preparing for the future from the first day may not be a priority. And by this I mean, the post-graduation life. I know I didn't start thinking about it until my sophomore year. In retrospect, I should've probably started

---

7 From Forbes website.

planning sooner.

McGraw-Hill Education's Future Workforce Survey revealed some statistics about recent graduates. Only 4 in 10 U.S. college students feel very or extremely prepared for their future careers. Many reported feeling like their college experience did not provide the critical skills they need to transit into the workforce, such as solving complex problems (43%), résumé writing (37%), interviewing (34%) and job searching (31%). While for the most part, they point to a grim post-college reality, there is something you can do for a better outcome.

Take advantage of your campus career resources. From job fairs, career advisers to résumé support and internships, there are so many campus career resources available. As a student, you need to be proactive in finding and using them.

Actively look for professional opportunities. Whether it be a season job, internship or volunteer gig, take every opportunity you come across to develop the skill set you'll need in the future. Finding these jobs will often require a proactive approach combined with patience, so carve out some time to do the work. Connect with other students to form a supportive network where you'll encourage each other.

Create your own opportunities. Don't limit yourself to internships or traditional jobs to acquire the experience you'll need when you join the workforce. In this digital age, anyone can start a successful venture with a few clicks and a good WiFi connection. Whether you start a blog, launch a photography business or take an online coding/marketing course, use part of your free time to give yourself opportunities with the same gains (more experience). This is key to not only practicing leadership, managing your time, connecting with new people, but also (and most importantly) honing a set of skills.

1. How many types of college students are mentioned in the first paragraph?

   A. Four.
   B. Five.
   C. Six.
   D. Seven.

2. What is the main idea of Paragraph 3?

   A. Figures show that employers worry about college students.
   B. Statistics show that college students are not adequately prepared for their career.

C. Statistics show that employers feel optimistic toward newly graduated students.

D. Figures show that college students are fully prepared for the future career success.

3. **Which skill is NOT included in college students' need to transit into the workforce?**

A. Solving complex problems.

B. Résumé writing.

C. Interviewing.

D. Communicating.

4. **What grade does sophomore refer to?**

A. The first year of college.

B. The second year of college.

C. The third year of college.

D. The forth year of college.

5. **Which one is true according to the passage?**

A. 3 in10 U.S. college students feel well prepared for their future careers.

B. Many reported feeling like their college experience provided the critical skills they need to transition into the workforce.

C. From job fairs, career advisers to résumé support and internships, there are few campus career resources available.

D. Finding jobs will often require a proactive approach combined with patience.

Passage two

Lifelong Learning Is Becoming an Economic Imperative[8]

NW: 292   **GL:** 12.4   **AWL percentage:** 8.01%
Keywords: lifelong learning; imperative; occupations

Technological change demands stronger and more continuous connections between education and employment, says Andrew Palmer. The faint outlines of such a system are now emerging.

In many occupations it has become essential to acquire new skills as established ones become <u>obsolete</u>. Burning Glass Technologies, a Boston-based startup that analyses labour markets by scraping data from online job advertisements, finds that the biggest demand is for new combinations of skills—what its boss, Matt Sigelman, calls "<u>hybrid jobs</u>". Coding skills, for example, are now being required well beyond the technology sector.

A college degree at the start of a working career does not answer the need for the continuous acquisition of new skills, especially as career spans are lengthening. Vocational training is good at giving people job-specific skills, but those, too, will need to be updated over and over again during a career lasting decade. Specific expertise is meant to be acquired on the job, but employers seem to have become less willing to invest in training their workforces. In Britain the average amount of training received by workers almost halved between 1997 and 2009, to just 0.69 hours a week.

Perhaps employers themselves are not sure what kind of expertise they need. But it could also be that training budgets are particularly vulnerable to cuts when the pressure is on. Changes in labour-market patterns may play a part too: Companies now have a broader range of options for getting the job done, from automation and offshoring to using self-employed workers and crowd-sourcing. "Organizations have moved from creating talent to consuming work," says Jonas Prising, the boss of Manpower, an employment consultancy.

Add all of this up, and it becomes clear that times have got tougher for workers of all kinds. A college degree is still a prerequisite for many jobs, but employers often do not trust it enough to hire workers just on the strength of that, without experience. In many occupations, workers on company payrolls face the prospect that their existing skills will become obsolete, yet it is often not obvious how they can gain new ones.

---

8 From The Economist website.

1. What does the underlined word "obsolete" (Line 2, Para. 2) refer to?

   A. Impossible.

   B. Out of date.

   C. Invisible.

   D. Fashionable.

2. What is the main idea of the third paragraph?

   A. A college degree is a must for most job applicants.

   B. Job-specific skills should be updated.

   C. Training of job-specific skills should be emphasized while employers have less will to do that.

   D. People can't find a job without a college degree.

3. What does the underlined phrase "hybrid jobs" (Line 4, Para. 2) mean?

   A. Professional jobs.

   B. Skillful jobs.

   C. Jobs requires mixed skills.

   D. Jobs requires single skill.

4. What is most employers' attitude toward job-expertise training according to the passage?

   A. Suspicious.

   B. Supportive.

   C. Opposed.

   D. Indifferent.

5. Which statement is true according to the passage?

   A. Career spans are shortening with the development of technology.

   B. Employers themselves are quite certain of what kind of expertise they need.

   C. The average amount of training received by workers increased in Britain.

   D. Workers are aware of their out-of-date skills, but they don't know how to gain new ones.

Reading Skills

Being an Active Reader

Active readers are fully engaged with a text, making connections and asking questions as they read. The following tips will help you be a more active reader.

1. Look at the title, headings, and photos. Use them to think about what you already know about the topic.

2. Circle any unfamiliar vocabulary. Write definitions in the text's margins.

3. Identify what each paragraph "says" (its main idea) and what it "does" (its purpose).

4. Connect ideas in the text. Notice words like "however", "importantly", and "finally".

5. Write any questions you have about the text in the margin.

6. Make word webs, outlines, or charts to help you understand ideas visually.

7. Summarize the text in one or two sentences.

8. Create exam questions about the text. Share and discuss them with a partner.

Exercises

Please read the above reading skill of being an active reader and use the guidelines to find some words connecting the ideas in Short Passage Two entitled "Lifelong Learning Is Becoming an Economic Imperative".

Words connecting ideas are: _____

THINK

Academic Words in Use

Fill in the blanks in the following sentences with the appropriate words provided in the box below. Change the form of the words if necessary.

like-minded	engine	cognitive	origin	educational	fulfilment
recycle	switch	trigger	fierce	acquire	feature

1. Collecting can be totally engrossing, and can give a strong sense of personal _____.
2. Another potential reason for postage stamps collecting is its _____ value.
3. Many collectors collect to develop their social life and keep contact with _____ people.
4. Research shows that bilingual experience may help to keep the _____ mechanisms sharp.
5. If the brain is a(n) _____, bilingualism may help it to go farther on some amount of fuel.
6. Bilinguals are often better at _____ between two tasks.
7. From our earliest _____, man has been making use of glass.
8. With growing consumers concerned for green issues, glass is an ideal material for _____.
9. Glass _____ in almost every aspect of human beings' life.
10. Glass making is a hi-tech industry operating in a(n) _____ competitive global market.
11. Listening to music can _____ the production of dopamine.
12. Mercury causes developmental delays in the _____ of language according to scientific research.

Writing

For this part, you are allowed 30 minutes to read the following paragraph and continue writing to make it a well-structured article. You should write at least 120 words but no more than 180 words.

On College Students' Career Planning

With the development of society, an increasing number of teenagers have opportunities to be educated. It is beneficial to our nation and society. However, problems of career planning arise with this phenomenon. More and more pressure on employment is exposed to college students. So a lot of colleges have paid more attention to college students' career planning. It seems that this phenomenon is becoming a trend.

Appendix: Video Script, Key and Sample Answers

Unit 1   Love

Video script

Love Is an Open Door

NW: 246   GL: 3.5   AWL percentage: 1.68%   Duration: 2′14″   WPM: 112

Anna: Elsa and I were really close when we were little, but then one day she just shut me out and I never knew why.

Hans: I would never shut you out.

Anna: Okay. Can I just say something crazy?

Hans: I love crazy.

Anna: All my life has been a series of doors in my face, and then suddenly I bumped into you.

Hans: I was thinking the same thing, because like I've been searching my whole life to find my own place, and maybe it's the party talking or the chocolate fondue.

Anna: But with you, with you.

Hans: I found my place.

Anna: I see your face.

Anna & Hans: And it's nothing like I've ever known before. Love is an open door… love is an open door… with you… with you… love is an open door.

Hans: I mean it's crazy.

Anna: What?

Hans: We finish each other's…

Anna: Sandwiches!

Hans: That's what I was gonna say.

Anna: I've never met someone who thinks so much like me.

Anna & Hans: Jinx… jinx again. Our mental synchronization can have but one explanation.

Hans: You…

Anna: And I…

Anna & Hans: … Were just meant to be.

Anna: Say goodbye.

Hans: Say goodbye.

Anna & Hans: … To the pain of the past. We don't have to feel it anymore. Love is an open door… love is an open door. Life can be so much more… with you…, love is am open… door.

Hans: Can I say something crazy…. Will you marry me?

Anna: Can I say something even crazier? Yes!

Key and sample answers

Viewing

Understanding the video clip

Anna	Hans
She and Elsa were close when they were young, but one day Elsa <u>shut her out</u>.	He was just <u>thinking</u> the same thing, because he had been <u>searching</u> his whole life.
She felt her life was <u>a series of</u> doors, then suddenly <u>bumped into</u> Hans.	He said they would <u>say goodbye</u> to the <u>pain</u> of the past.
With Hans she found <u>her place</u>, she saw <u>his face</u>.	He felt love can be so <u>much more</u> with her.
Anna thought their <u>mental</u> synchronization can have but one <u>explanation</u>.	At last, he asked <u>Anna to marry him</u>.
Finally, Anna say something even <u>crazier</u>, yes.	

Further thoughts

Advantages	Disadvantages
1. full of enthusiasm	1. not lasting for a long time
2. arousing the inside power instantly	2. always hurtful
3. attracted by his/her superficial quality	3. without deep understanding
4. the feeling of "meant to be" being so great	4. unreliable
5. having strong romantic love feeling	5. easily be cheated, especially the girls

Banked Cloze

1-5 JIFOC 6-10 KEAND

Long Passage

1-5 NEBHK 6-10 GLJIM

Short Passages

Passage one 1-5 CCDBB
Passage two 1-5 ADCBC

Reading Skills

Transitional elements are: because, or, like, and, also, that is, such is, but

Academic Words in Use

1. traditional   2. shifted   3. perspective   4. purchase   5. aware
6. survey   7. significantly   8. reveals   9. priority   10. legal
11. generation   12. conducted

Writing

Sample writing

Do You Want to Celebrate Valentine's Day?

Valentine's day is approaching and people in many parts of the world are getting ready to lighten their wallets for their loved ones. Eating out, buying presents, chocolates or flowers for their significant others have become a tradition on this particular day. It is definitely the day of love in the world and has also spread its roots to every corner of the earth.

Originally, Valentine's day was celebrated in the West to honor Saint Valentine from Rome, who was imprisoned and executed for performing illegal weddings for persecuted Christians. But nowadays it has become a special day for sellers, who eagerly look forward to an increase in sales on this day.

Valentine's day has completely changed into a commercial event that you need to prove your love by gifts and flowers. On that day the flower prices soar like a rocket. All the restaurants and theaters are filled with people. You need to wait for quite a long time to have dinner in a nice restaurant, let alone some fancy places you need to book them several weeks in advance. It is hard to enjoy the romance with your lover. Sometimes it even leads to unexpected conflicts between the couple.

Valentine's day is supposed to be an occasion to express love and should not fall into a commercial event. A home-made dinner carries more weight than expensive flowers on this day in many people's heart, so there are increasingly less people to celebrate this day.

Unit 2 Growing Up

Video script

Do Grades Matter?

NW: 449   GL: 8.0   AWL percentage: 5.41%   Duration: 3′28″   WPM: 129

Are you stressed about grades? Should you be? That's such a weighted question.

Most of a person's young life revolves around school, waking up every day at the crack of dawn, carrying an ungodly amount of books, and working towards good grades that will theoretically help them get into a good college and a good job. Students are constantly asking, "Do good grades actually matter?" "Is my life predetermined by the grades I get in school?"

"I think they matter in a sense, but I don't think people should be obsessed with them and think that they measure intelligence."

"I should have done better in school. Probably would have made things a lot easier."

"OK, I think I guess high school grades matter because they get you into college. College grades don't matter."

A 2013 NPR poll found that nearly 40% of parents believed their high schooler feels high levels of school related stress. Some symptoms of grade anxiety might be increased heart rate, sweating, and decreased appetite. Being a kid should be fun, right?

The National Institute of Mental Health reports that anxiety in children and young adults has been increasing since the 1950s. According to some researchers, the increase in standardized testing may contribute to this.

The SAT is the subject of millions of high schooler's little malleable minds, always there over their heads like some sort of dark cloud filled with math. You know what I mean. This also begs the question, do standardized tests truly measure intelligence?

"Oh God, no. Like the thing is, I consider myself a pretty intelligent dude, and I just got an average score on the SATs, so I think there's something wrong with the SAT."

"The SAT's bad because it measures how well you can take a test rather than how much intelligence you actually have."

One school of thought is that these tests are unable to account for important areas, like critical thinking, collaboration, and imagination. Will memorizing vocabulary entitle you to a better future? According to a survey by the National Association of Colleges and Employers, 78.3% of employers claim to screen future employees by GPA. However, 63.5% of employers only use a 3.0 as a GPA cutoff for employment. So, pushing yourself to be above average may not mean much in the long run.

There's also the worry that schools are formulating their curriculums around the test. This is believed to be a result of incentive systems put in place by the Department of Education that rewards schools with higher test scores. A proposal by New York governor Andrew Cuomo would have 50% of a teacher's evaluation correlate to the result of their student's scores.

Education should be fluid and expressive, tailored to student's needs and wants, not based around a system of points. What if you just want to paint some stuff or write some stuff?

So, do grades matter? Yes and no. If you're looking to pursue a path of higher education, then yeah, they do matter. But don't stress about grades. Everyone's path is different, and chances are you won't even remember your SAT score in five years. Whatever you focus on, just try, to the best of your ability, whatever that may be. The amount of effort you put into something will always say more than a letter on a report card.

Key and sample answers

Viewing

Understanding the video clip

Questions	Opinions and facts
1. Do good grades actually matter?	Most of a person's young life <u>revolves</u> around school, waking up every day at the crack of <u>dawn</u>, carrying an ungodly amount of books, and working towards good grades that will <u>theoretically</u> help them get into a good college and a good job. Students are constantly asking, "Do good grades actually matter?" "Is my life <u>predetermined</u> by the grades I get in school?"
2. What are the results of NPR poll?	A 2013 NPR poll found that nearly <u>40%</u> of parents believed their high schooler feels high levels of <u>school related</u> stress. Some <u>symptoms</u> of grade anxiety might be increased heart rate, <u>sweating</u>, and decreased appetite. Being a kid should be fun, right?
3. Can tests be able to account for important areas, like critical thinking?	One school of thought is that these tests are unable to <u>account</u> for important areas, like critical thinking, <u>collaboration</u>, and imagination. Will memorizing vocabulary <u>entitle</u> you to a better future? According to a survey by the National Association of Colleges and Employers, 78.3% of employers claim to <u>screen</u> future employees by GPA. However, 63.5% of employers <u>only</u> use a 3.0 as a GPA cutoff for employment. So, pushing yourself to be above average may not mean much in the long run.
4. What is people's another worry?	There's also the worry that schools are <u>formulating</u> their curriculums around the test. This is believed to be <u>a result</u> of incentive systems put in place by the Department of Education that <u>rewards</u> schools with higher test scores. A <u>proposal</u> by New York governor Andrew Cuomo would have 50% <u>of</u> a teacher's <u>evaluation</u> correlate to the result of their student's scores.
5. What is real education?	Education should be <u>fluid</u> and expressive, <u>tailored</u> to student's needs and wants, not based around a system of <u>points</u>. What if you just want to paint some stuff or write some stuff?

6. So, do grades matter?	Yes and no. If you're looking to pursue a path of higher education, then yeah, they do matter. But don't stress about grades. Everyone's path is different, and chances are you won't even remember your SAT score in five years. Whatever you focus on, just try to the best of your ability, whatever that may be. The amount of effort you put into something will always say more than a letter on a report card.

Further thoughts

Yes	No
1. Grade can be the most effective way for selecting talents.	1. Grade does not measure a person's intelligence, creativity and critical thinking.
2. Grade can indicate the effort people put into the thing in concern.	2. Grade is just one dimension of a whole person.
3. Grade is one of ways to quantify a person's ability to learn.	3. A person's comprehensive ability cannot be seen by his/her grades.
4. Quantification by scores is a relatively fair way to compete.	4. Due to various irresistible factors, such as personal psychological status and the influence of external environment, it is slightly unfair to evaluate talents by scores.
5. It can give students more access to better study resources.	5. Grade is not everything. If you focus on grade only, your other abilities cannot be exercised.
6. Good grades give people a sense of achievement and inspire people to make progress.	6. Desperate pursuit of high grades may get you lost.
7. For teachers, grades can help them know their students better. Teachers can be targeted to explain where students' scores are generally low.	7. Teachers will inevitably treat students with different grades differently, which will make some students who do not understand the teacher's good intentions full of negative emotions.

Banked Cloze

1-5 JACIB **6-10** DEOKM

Long Passage

1-5 DEFGH **6-10** IJKLM

Short Passages

Passage one 1-5 BDACA
Passage two 1-5 ADBBD

Reading Skills

Patterns of development:

1. the phenomenon of stress and anxiety
2. the causes of stress and anxiety
3. how to reduce stress and anxiety
4. what method is best for different people

Academic Words in Use

1. technical
2. appraisal
3. perspective
4. efficient
5. appealing
6. self-conscious
7. alternation
8. positive
9. prescription
10. symptoms
11. specific
12. ultimately

Writing

Sample writing

What Is Your Definition of Personal Growth?

Personal growth is the collection of knowledge, practices, and tools that an individual relies on while striving for the ultimate goal of personal betterment and self-actualization.

Personal growth is first and foremost about seeing all of your traits as traits, not flaws. The age-old question "Who am I?" is where personal growth starts for many people. Being self-aware is possibly the most important aspect of personal growth. Having a deep understanding of oneself is crucial if one wants to improve.

Personal growth is a lifelong solitary pursuit towards self-actualization. It's about knowing that perfection cannot be obtained, yet striving for it anyway; and that ultimate success comes not from the destination, but the journey. It's about having the personal fortitude to recognize that there are no magical "one weird trick" solutions and that achieving your dreams and goals takes hard work and perseverance.

Personal growth means different things to different people. In general, it refers to the self-improvement of your skills, knowledge, personal qualities, life goals and outlook. Whenever you seek to better yourself in any way—be it your temperament, your formal education, or your maturity, you are seeking personal growth.

Unit 3 University Culture

Video script

How to Balance College and Life

NW: 544 GL: 8.1 AWL percentage: 5.92% Duration: 2'44" WPM: 199

It's very hard to find ways to keep up with all of your college work and still keep a balanced life. Many people say that when you get into college you need to choose from two vortices while sacrificing the third one. Well, I need to tell you that that's completely not true. If you plan and organize your life, you'll be able to manage your sleep schedule, your studying sessions and your night outs without sacrificing one of them.

The first thing you need to do is being realistic. Instead of sleeping 9 hours a day perhaps you'll need to cut back to 7 hours a day, which will probably provide enough energy throughout the day without letting you feel the burnouts. On the other hand, you need to ration the time you spend with your friends and family. The best way to do so is scheduling a fixed time to be with them and dedicate yourself 100% to them. It's not how much time you have available that matters. What matters is what you do with the time you have available. Cutting back on fundamental aspects of your life will really hurt your grades. And if it doesn't hurt your grades right away, it will hurt your body and state of mind sooner than you think. Sleepless nights have a mark on your body. On the other hand, depriving yourself of the time spent with your loved ones can hurt and destroy relationships, and in the end of the day you'll find out that those grades aren't worth as much as that.

Another thing I recommend is finding some sort of physical activity that helps you manage energy levels. Even running ten minutes a day will do wonders for your physical and mental health, letting you cope with high stress levels and the feeling of burnout.

You also need to prioritize. Having a heavily crowded schedule just for the sake of it will result in lower grades and the lower ability to focus on those classes. Big classes and courses that you think you can personally enjoy can also help you on your chosen career path. Try to keep both of those aspects in mind when you're picking subjects for the next semester or else risking signing up for classes that are just filling you with stress, and won't even matter when you get your diploma.

Find a way to get help. You are not alone in this path and many of your classmates are probably feeling the same way. Try to get together and find a way to share some tasks or somehow trade notes and materials to help each other. If you can't attend the lecture for any reason, don't hesitate to ask for the class notes and assignment. Finding a reading group is great to divide huge books into manageable chunks and distribute them between the members, so you have less reading to do and are able to summarize your part in a better way and then share your summary with your colleagues.

Schedule some "me" time. Don't look at your personal space as a failure towards your productivity goals. Try to incorporate at least half an hour with yourself in your busy schedule and stick to it religiously.

Key and sample answers

Viewing

Understanding the video clip

Ways to balance college and life	Details
1. Be realistic.	Instead of sleeping 9 hours a day perhaps you'll need to <u>cut back</u> to 7 hours a day, which will probably provide enough energy throughout the day without letting you feel the burnouts. On the other hand, you need to ration the time you spend with your friends and family. The best way to do so is scheduling a fixed time to be with them and dedicate yourself 100% to them. It's not how much time you have available that matters. What matters is what you do with the time we have available. Cutting back on fundamental aspects of your life will really hurt your grades. And if it doesn't hurt your grades right away, it will hurt your body and <u>state of mind</u> sooner than you think. Sleepless nights have a mark on your body. On the other hand, depriving yourself of the time spent with your loved ones can hurt and destroy relationships, and in the end of the day you'll find out that those grades aren't worth as much as that.
2. Find some sort of physical activity that helps you manage energy levels.	Even running ten minutes a day will do wonders for your <u>physical and mental health</u>, letting you cope with high stress levels and the feeling of burnout.
3. Prioritize.	Having a heavily crowded schedule just for the sake of it will result in lower grades and the lower ability <u>to focus on those classes</u>. Big classes and courses that you think you can personally enjoy can also help you on your chosen career path. Try to keep both of those aspects in mind when you're picking subjects for the next semester or else risking signing up for classes that are just <u>filling you with stress</u>, and won't even matter when you get your diploma.

4. Find a way to get help.	You are not alone in this path and many of your classmates are probably <u>feeling the same way</u>. Try to get together and find a way to share some tasks or somehow trade notes and materials to help each other. If you can't attend the lecture for any reason, don't hesitate to ask for <u>the class notes and assignment</u>. Finding a reading group is great to divide huge books into manageable chunks and <u>distribute them between the members,</u> so you have less reading to do and are able to summarize your part in a better way and then share your summary with your colleagues.
5. Schedule some "me" time.	Don't look at your personal space as <u>a failure toward your productivity goals</u>. Try to incorporate at least half an hour with yourself in your busy schedule and stick to it religiously.

Further thoughts

Other ways	Reasons
1. Create a morning routine	1. Create a routine around a daily morning practice, such as meditating or waking up a half-hour early to get work done before ever checking your email. By sticking to this morning after morning, you'll automatically begin your workday on a positive note, with a sense of accomplishment.
2. Set aside quiet time	2. Carving out some time for yourself is essential to stay grounded. Whether you squeeze in time to call a friend or just sit and decompress sans electronic devices, designating uninterrupted time (however short!) to clear your head can work wonders for your mood and will help you to think more clearly when things are moving fast.
3. Make room for creativity	3. Making time for creative expression—whatever that looks like for you—will help stay centered when it feels like work is taking over your life. It allows you to channel stress, anger, resentment, or whatever other negative emotions you may be holding onto in a productive, healthy way.
4. Join or create a study group	4. One way to balance your school life and your social life is by forming a study group where you can hang out with friends and study together. This may not be ideal for everyone, but it's a good way to not miss out on any part of the college experience. You can take breaks during the study session to chat and have a snack, and spend the rest of the time focusing on your work.
5. Let go of perfectionism	5. It's easier to maintain that perfectionist habit as a kid, but as you grow up, life gets more complicated. As you climb the ladder at work and as your family grows, your responsibilities mushroom. Perfectionism becomes out of reach, and if that habit is left unchecked, it can become destructive.

Banked Cloze

1-5 FKDHB **6-10** JOGCM

Long Passage

1-5 JBEAG **6-10** IFIHL

Short Passages

Passage one 1-5 ACDBA

Passage two 1-5 BACAD

Reading Skills

Computers can help people in different ways. Take science work as an example. Computers help scientists in analyzing data and doing complex calculation. Computers, for another example, are very useful in multi-media classrooms. Besides, computers may also play a great role in helping children with their lesson. Whatever you are doing, you may find computers a useful aid.

Academic Words in Use

1. lecturer
2. stress
3. aspects
4. mental
5. colleagues
6. schedule
7. assignments
8. grades
9. focus
10. energy
11. available
12. goals

Writing

Sample writing

My View on the Postgraduate Craze

Every year, millions of college students sit in for the postgraduate entrance examination. More and more students have regarded the pursuing of a master degree as an indispensable part of their education. What is to account for their enthusiasm for a postgraduate diploma?

First, it is the demand of the time. In an age of knowledge updating and information explosion, what you have learned in college can hardly meet the demands of society. Talents of high quality who are equipped with the latest knowledge and skill will be needed more than ever. That is why many students will further their studies.

Second, we all recognize that the more education we have, the more likely we are to succeed. Compared with those without a master degree, masters will enjoy more preferential treatment, for example, better salaries, more opportunities for promotion and training. A postgraduate diploma can guarantee a more promising career.

Last but not least, with the graduation of a large number of college students, competition for jobs becomes more and more fierce. One way to gain some advantages over others is to have a higher degree. No wonder millions of students consider pursuing postgraduate studies as a necessity.

Unit 4   Lifestyles I like

Video script

Maintaining a Healthy Balanced Lifestyle

NW: 561   GL: 8.6   AWL percentage: 3.29%   Duration: 3′18″   WPM: 170

From the moment we wake up, we're faced with decisions. Should we walk to work or drive, take a packed lunch or grab something on the go? With so many choices in so little time, it isn't surprising that we don't always think whether the decisions we make through the day add up to a healthy lifestyle, including a balanced diet.

Kicking off the day with a nutritious breakfast is a good place to start. Why? When we wake up, our body has been without food for a number of hours, so we need to eat something to give us the energy to function. From walking and talking through two critical functions such as breathing and pumping blood around our body, even thinking requires energy, so breakfast and food generally is pretty important. There are other benefits too. Evidence shows that those who eat breakfast are generally slimmer than those who skip it. And children who eat breakfast concentrate more and perform better at school.

Our brain requires around 130 grams of glucose, which is a type of sugar per day to keep functioning. You'll find glucose in all sorts of foods from fruit and vegetables to honey. So for a healthy start to your day and to get that early morning energy boost, how about enjoying some porridge with raisins or maybe a small glass of orange juice and a bowl of whole grain cereal. Today, more and more of us are eating on-the-go than ever before. This can make it more difficult to track the calories we're eating as we go with the added extras or grabbing a coffee with our sandwich.

Nutritional labels can help us keep track of how we're doing. They include lots of useful information from the calorie content to the different ingredients including the amount of total sugars. Did you know that when it comes to sugars our bodies do not distinguish between them whether natural or added in the home or used in manufacturing? So the sucrose in an apple is broken down in exactly the same way as the sucrose in your sugar bowl. As our energy levels dip through the day, it can be tempting to reach for a mid-afternoon snack. Snacks can make up to 20% of our daily calorie intake. So think about how snacks can complement the other foods you've eaten through the day. It's also worth thinking about how your snacks can help you get one of your five a day.

A couple of ways to look after yourself includes keeping an eye on what you're eating and leading an active lifestyle. The UK government recommends 150 minutes of moderate exercise or 75 minutes of more vigorous exercise for adults each week. As you approach dinner, take a moment to think about the food you've eaten through the day. No single food or drink contains all the essential nutrients your body needs. Also think about the number of calories you've consumed and how active you've been.

Finally, don't forget that drinks also count towards your daily calorie allowance so that small glass of white wine or a pint of beer shouldn't be forgotten when totting up your total intake for the day.

Whatever choices you make during the day, take a moment to think about how making even the smallest of changes could make a big difference.

Key and sample answers

Viewing

Understanding the video clip

Suggestions	Details
1. A nutritious breakfast	Kicking off the day with a nutritious breakfast is a good place to start. Why? When we <u>wake up</u>, our body has been without food for a number of hours, so we need to eat something to give us the <u>energy to function</u>. From walking and talking through two critical functions such as breathing and pumping blood around our body, even thinking requires energy, so breakfast and food generally is pretty important. There are other benefits too. Evidence shows that those who eat breakfast <u>are generally slimmer</u> than those who skip it. And children who eat breakfast concentrate more and perform better at school.

2. Right amount of sugar	Our brain requires around 130 grams of glucose, which is a type of sugar per day <u>to keep functioning</u>. You'll find glucose in all sorts of foods from fruit and vegetables to honey. So for a healthy start to your day and to get that early morning energy boost, how about enjoying some porridge with raisins or maybe a small glass of orange juice and <u>a bowl of whole grain cereal</u>. Today, more and more of us are eating on-the-go than ever before. This can make it more difficult to <u>track the calories</u> we're eating as we go with the added extras or grabbing a coffee with our sandwich.
3. Nutritional labels	Nutritional labels can help us <u>keep track of</u> how we're doing. They include lots of useful information from the calorie content to the different ingredients including the amount of total sugars. Did you know that <u>when it comes to</u> sugars our bodies do not distinguish between them whether natural or added in the home or used in manufacturing? So the sucrose in an apple is broken down <u>in exactly the same way</u> as the sucrose in your sugar bowl. As our energy levels dip through the day, it can be tempting to reach for a mid-afternoon snack. Snacks can make up to 20% of our daily calorie intake. So think about how snacks can complement the other foods you've eaten through the day. It's also worth thinking about how your snacks can help you get one of your five a day.
4. Look after yourself	A couple of ways to look after yourself includes <u>keeping an eye on</u> what you're eating and leading an active lifestyle. The UK government recommends 150 minutes of moderate exercise or 75 minutes of more vigorous exercise for adults each week. As you approach dinner, <u>take a moment</u> to think about the food you've eaten through the day. No single food or drink contains all the essential nutrients your body needs. Also think about the number of calories you've consumed and how active you've been.
5. Be careful with drinks	Finally, don't forget that drinks also count towards your daily calorie allowance so that small glass of white wine or a pint of beer shouldn't be forgotten when totting up <u>your total intake</u> for the day.

Further thoughts

Unhealthy lifestyles	Healthy lifestyles
1. Eat too much meat and a few vegetables.	1. Eat a lot of fresh fruits and vegetables.
2. Stay up late.	2. Have a good night sleep.
3. Sit by the desk all daylong.	3. Take moderate regular exercise.
4. Drink ten cups of coffee a day.	4. Prefer drinks that doesn't contain caffeine or too much sugar.
5. Smoke two packages of cigarettes a day.	5. Neither smoke nor drink alcohol.

Banked Cloze

1-5 HLJDF   6-10 KBAGI

Long Passage

1-5 GEHKN   6-10 DJLBI

Short Passages

Passage one 1-5 CABDA
Passage two 1-5 DCBCC

Reading Skills

Purpose: In writing the passage the writer intends to inform the reader of an alarming fact that the aspects of our social life have been greatly influenced by our preference for endless entertainment.

Academic Words in Use

1. rely
2. issue
3. survived
4. challenges
5. previous
6. individual
7. jobs
8. philosopher
9. Despite
10. physical
11. majority
12. editor

Writing

Sample writing

Live a Healthy Life

A healthy lifestyle is not only a way to avoid risks, but also a chance to live well and happily. Once you choose to live a healthy life, it lasts all your life. It not only helps you live longer and better but also let you be less prone to sickness and diseases. A healthy lifestyle is the kind of lifestyle that we should all strive for.

Having a healthy lifestyle is all about choosing to live your life in the healthiest way possible. There are a few things you have to do to start living your life in a healthy way.

This means doing a moderate amount of exercise daily, such as jogging, yoga, boxing, etc. In addition, you must also have a balanced and nutritional diet with all the food groups. It would be best if you were taking the right amount of proteins, vitamins, minerals, and fats to help you have a proper diet.

All in all, when we do all the necessary things to have a healthy lifestyle, our lives are going on the right path.

Unit 5　Emotion & Interaction

Video script

Discipline Your Emotion

NW: 617　**GL:** 4.7　**AWL percentage:** 5.48%　**Duration:** 3′37″　**WPM:** 171

You can't connect the dots looking forward, you can only connect them looking backwards.

So you have to trust that the dots will somehow connect in your future. You have to trust in something, your gut, destiny, life, karma whatever. Because believing that the dots will connect down the road will give you the confidence to follow your heart. Even when it leads you off the well-worn path. And that will make all the difference. Your time is limited, so don't waste it living someone else's life. Don't be trapped by dogma, which is living with the results of other people's thinking. Don't let the noise of others' opinions drown out your own inner voice. You've got to find what you love. And that is as true for your work as it is for your lovers. Your work is going to fill a large part of your life and the only way to be truly satisfied is to do what you believe is great work. And the only way to do great work is to love what you do. If you haven't found it yet, keep looking and don't settle. Have the courage to follow your heart and intuition. They somehow already know what you truly want to become.

You're going to have some ups and you're going to have some downs. Most people give up on themselves easily. You know the human spirit is powerful. There is nothing as powerful…—it's hard to kill the human spirit! Anybody can feel good when they have their health, their bills are paid, they have happy relationships. Anybody can have a larger vision. Then anybody can have faith under those kinds of circumstances. The real challenge of growth mentally, emotionally and spiritually comes when you get knocked down. It takes courage to act. Part of being hungry when you have been defeated. It takes courage to start over again.

Fear kills dreams. Fear kills hope. Fear put people in the hospital. Fear can age you. Fear can hold you back from doing something that you know within yourself that you are capable of doing, but it will paralyze you. At the end of your feelings is nothing, but at the end of every principle is a promise. Behind your little feelings, it might not be absolutely nothing at the end of your little feelings. But behind every principle is a promise. And some of you in your life, the reason why you are not at your goal right now, because you are just all about your feelings. All on your feelings, you don't feel like waking up. So who does? Don't allow your emotion to control you. We are emotional but you want to begin to discipline your emotion. If you don't discipline and contain your emotion, they will use you. You want it, and you're going to go all out to have it. It's not going to be easy, when you want to change. It's not easy. If it were in fact easy, everybody would do it. But if you're serious, you'll go all out. I'm in control here. I'm not going to let this get me down. I'm not going to let this destroy me. I'm coming back. And I'll be stronger and better because of it! You have got to make a declaration. That this is what you stand for! You're standing up for your dreams. You're standing up for peace of mind. You're standing up for health. Take full responsibility for your life. Accept where you are and the responsibility that you're going to take yourself where you want to go. You can decide that I'm going to live each day as if it were my last!

Key and sample answers

Viewing

Understanding the video clip

1. Don't waste your time living other people's life.	1. We need to believe the dots will connect the road, will give your the <u>confidence</u> to <u>follow</u> your heart. Don't let the <u>noise</u> of others' <u>opinions</u> drown out your own <u>inner voice</u>.
2. Work will be a great part of life.	2. Your work is gonna fill a large part of your life and the only way to be <u>truly satisfied</u> is to do what you <u>believe is great work</u>, and the only way to do great work is to love what you do.
3. Don't give up easily.	3. Most people give up on themselves easily. You know the <u>human spirit is powerful</u>. The real challenge of growth <u>mentally, emotionally</u> and <u>spiritually</u> comes when you get knocked down.

4. Don't be afraid of fear.	4. Fear can hold you back from doing something that you know <u>within yourself</u> that you're <u>capable of</u> doing, but it will paralyze you.
5. Be the master of your emotion.	5. Don't allow your emotions to control you. We are <u>emotional</u> but you want to begin to <u>discipline your emotion</u>. It's not easy. If it were in fact easy, everybody would do it. But if you're serious, you'll go all out. You're standing up for your <u>dreams</u>. You're standing up for <u>peace of mind</u>. You're standing up for <u>health</u>.

Further thoughts

Pros	Cons
1. As a person, I have the right to express my emotion.	1. Personal emotion is a private thing.
2. Only after I release the bad emotion, I can feel happy.	2. Don't let other people see your worst side. It is a good way to protect yourself.
3. Just because I'm in public and no one knows me, I don't care how people think about me.	3. Take a deep breath, and then you will know there isn't a big deal at all.
4. I am just a normal people, and I will be vulnerable when things go wrong. Releasing my bad emotion is good for my mental health.	4. You will feel regret that you lost control of your emotion.
5. I don't want to be a "fake" person.	5. It is a process to become mature.

Banked Cloze

1-5 DBJKO 6-10 LIFNA

Long Passage

1-5 JGAFK 6-10 BEDLH

Short Passages

Passage one 1-5 BBDBD
Passage two 1-5 CBADB

Reading Skills

Sequencing order: cause and effect

The cause: The old doesn't have enough friends and family nearby.

The effect: They are at risk of depression.

The cause: An intergenerational program is undergoing in some places.

The effect: Both the old and the young feel happy.

The cause: Being involved with the children makes the seniors feel useful and happy.

The effect: The seniors' overall mental and physical health may improve.

Academic Words in Use

1. depressed
2. benefited
3. exposed
4. ranged
5. communicate
6. community
7. expansion
8. mental
9. location
10. environmental
11. response
12. features

Writing

Sample writing

Should Emotions Be Taught in Schools?

Who taught you how to identify and manage your emotions, how to recognize them when they arose and how to navigate your way through them? For may adults, the answer is: No one. You hacked your way through those confusing thickets on your own.

Recently, a number of researchers believe emotional skills should rank as high in importance in children's education as math, reading, history and science.

Why should we empathize the emotion education? Because research has found that people who are emotionally skilled perform better in school, have better relationships with teachers and classmates, and engage less in unhealthy behaviors, such as committing suicide, hurting themselves or other people, emotional depression and so on. In our education system, kids are taught to study hard instead of having a sound emotion, so their emotional problems are often ignored. In fact, emotions can give us valuable information about the world, but we are often taught or socialized not to listen to them. So, we always tend to hide our emotions, especially the feelings of shame. It is necessary to help kids understand their emotions and find a positive way to deal with them. Emotion accompanies us every day, whether we are aware of it or not. Therefore, we should teach the kids how to face the emotional ups and downs, instead of being slave to them.

Unit 6   Cooperation and Conflict

Video script

What Is a Cooperative?

NW: 255   **GL:** 9.4   **AWL percentage:** 3.77%   **Duration:** 1′50″   **WPM:** 139

Ownership matters. It gives people a say in the things they care about. Being an owner in a business, for example, gives people motivation and a stake in its success. But over the last thirty years, the number of people who have control over the businesses that shape our lives has become smaller, not larger. It's no surprise that when you ask them, people say they have no influence: no influence in their workplace, over the businesses and over the economy as a whole. Cooperatives, however, offer a solution. From the outside they may look like any other business, but inside they are very different. They're owned in control together by the people closest to the business: employees, customers, residents, suppliers, not distant shareholders. They have an equal say in how the business is run and they even decide what to do with the profits. And cooperatives work. There are nearly 7,000 independent co-ops in the UK. They're found in every sector, from high street retailers to farmer control businesses, cooperative pubs and credit unions. Some of our most famous brands come from cooperatives, from champagne and parmesan to Lurpak butter and BirdsEye peas. Even Barcelona Football Club is a co-op owned by expands. Co-ops contribute 37 billion pounds each year to the British economy and boost UK productivity innovation and entrepreneurship. And they work for the 15 million members who together own the UK's co-ops. Cooperatives give people, in fact all of us, more control over the things that matter. What do you want to do together?

Key and sample answers

Viewing

Understanding the video clip

1. Why cooperative is necessary?	Being an owner in a business gives people <u>motivation</u> and a <u>stake</u> in its success. But over the last thirty years, the number of people who <u>have control over</u> the businesses that <u>shape our lives</u> has become smaller. It's no surprise people say they have no influence: no influence <u>in their workplace</u>, over the business and <u>over the economy</u> as a whole. Cooperatives offer a solution.
2. What is a cooperative?	Cooperatives are owned in control together by the people <u>closest to the business</u>: employees, customers, <u>residents</u>, suppliers, not <u>distant shareholders</u>. They have <u>an equal say</u> in how the business is run and they even decide <u>what to do with the profits</u>.
3. What are the benefits of cooperatives?	There are nearly 7,000 <u>independent</u> co-ops in the UK. They're found in every sector, from <u>high street retailer</u> to <u>farmer control businesses</u>, cooperative pubs and <u>credit unions</u>. Co-ops contribute 37 billion pounds each year to the British economy and boost UK <u>productivity innovation and entrepreneurship</u>. Cooperatives give all of us more control over <u>the things that matter</u>.

Further thoughts

Pros of cooperative	Cons of cooperative
1. It can reduce business risks.	1. It has fewer incentives for large investors.
2. It can enable a large purchase in a group.	2. It is time-consuming for making decisions.
3. This equitable type of organization makes the cooperative business a lot more stable.	3. Most cooperative businesses do not have professional managers because they are just too expensive.
4. It is more autonomous compared to business controlled by their investors.	4. With a cooperative, the lack of profit incentive may lead to lack of interest.
5. It can boost its members not only economically but also morally and socially.	5. Cooperative sometimes also has problems when it tries to get debt capital from banks and other financial institutions.

Banked Cloze

1-5 FKEBH   6-10 OLNDC

Long Passage

1-5 JJDBK   6-10 EDDCE

Short Passages

Passage one 1-5 ADDCB
Passage two 1-5 CDCBD

Reading Skills

1-5 OFFOO

Academic Words in Use

1. immense   2. tackling   3. fulfilled   4. expected   5. instilled
6. minimum   7. solutions   8. capture   9. available   10. significant
11. privileged 12. overwhelmingly

Writing

Sample writing

Competition or Cooperation, a Dilemma?

Today, many people believe that it is vital to cultivate the spirit of competitiveness in early childhood education. Parents always say that life is a constant battle and one has to be competitive to emerge out of it successfully. However, some argue that the competition could also lead to negative outcomes, thus cooperation and teamwork spirit should be encouraged instead.

In my view, the two views should not be contradictory, and it is important for us to examine both sides to reach a sound conclusion.

Encouraging children to be more competitive involves a recognition that they will face increasingly fierce competition in the future, and we should prepare them in the early stage of their lives. Competitiveness is also a highly motivating force, for instance, in their studies, as no one wants to lag behind others. Nevertheless, some fear that children would become indifferent and selfish with too much competition in their education.

In this sense, helping children learn how to cooperate with their peers could compensate for this tendency. In fact, children can cultivate leadership and teamwork spirit through group discussion and group work, and they are less likely to become overly self-centered. However, some others worry that children will become less independent if they are used to relying on cooperation to get things done. This, to me, is where appropriate guidance from teachers is needed to avoid extremes.

To sum up, it is safe to say that both competition and cooperation are needed in children's education today, and teachers should play an active role in helping children pursue a balance between the two aspects.

Unit 7 Entrepreneurship

Video script

How to Be an Entrepreneur?

NW: 502   GL: 12   AWL percentage: 4.12%   Duration: 3′24″   WPM: 148

Many of us want to become entrepreneurs. Starting your own business is one of the biggest dreams of our times, but how do you get to be an entrepreneur? Most of the advice focuses on the practicalities: writing a business plan, raising money, finding staff, marketing and PR. We'll go down a different route. In our eyes, at the heart of successful entrepreneurship lies something oddly more abstract and accurate insight into the causes of human unhappiness. To be an entrepreneur means essentially to become an expert in the things that make life difficult for people. That's because every properly ambitious business is in some way trying to fix things for other people. And the bigger and more original what you're trying to fix happens to be, the more successful your business can be, because consumer society is now well developed.

It may be easy to think that all the big problems out there already have thousands of fixes anyway. Think of all those car companies or pizza outlets or news websites, we surely have enough of everything. What could we possibly add to what's already out there? But to get a sense of the vast opportunities that still remain in capitalism, all you need to do is ask yourself where and in what areas you're unhappy in the course of an average day. Every unhappiness is really a new business waiting to be born. Your frustrations are a nearly inexhaustible source of raw materials out of which the businesses of the future can be built. So, while there may already be plenty of breakfast cereals and T-shirts and cellphones and cab rides for sale, there's so much more that frustrates and depresses us. Think of how difficult it is to get on with one's partner, educate children, cope with anxiety, discover what you want to do with your life, find a nice place to live, calm down in the evening.

One could go on and on. Our griefs and irritations are endless. Thankfully, for the budding entrepreneurs, the biggest first step to take towards entrepreneurship is therefore to learn to study your own unhappiness and what might possibly heal it for you and others. When profits decline in businesses, it's really the result of too many people throwing themselves at trying to fix the same area, because they can't think of anything more innovative to do rather than start a new airline mobile phone company or supermarket chain. And by contrast, healthy profits are a reward for understanding and mastering an area of human distress ahead of anyone else. Of course, ideas aren't enough on their own. You need to take care of practicalities and money, but they won't help you if your original psychological insight into human unhappiness isn't sound. And by the same token, if your insight into what makes people unhappy is razor sharp and your solutions are bold, then, however difficult the journey, your business will stand a high chance of making money and benefit in humanity, too.

Key and sample answers

Viewing

Understanding the video clip

How do you get to be an entrepreneur? Most of the advice focuses on 1. <u>practicalities</u>.
At the heart of successful entrepreneurship lies something oddly more abstract and 2. <u>accurate insight</u> into the causes of human unhappiness.
The bigger and more 3. <u>original</u> what you're trying to fix happens to be, the more successful your business can be, because 4. <u>consumer society</u> is now well developed.

One could go on and on. Our griefs and 5. <u>irritations</u> are endless.	
However difficult the journey, your business will 6. <u>stand a high chance of</u> making money and benefit in humanity, too.	

Further thoughts

Advice of starting up a business	Something that may frustrate and depress us (Entrepreneurship opportunities)
1. writing a business plan	1. getting on with one's partner
2. raising money	2. educating children
3. finding staff	3. coping with anxiety
4. marketing	4. discovering what you want to do with your life
5. PR	5. finding a nice place to live
	6. calming down in the evening

Banked Cloze

1-5 LBGJM   6-10 INKEH

Long Passage

1-5 IKJGE   6-10 FCBKD

Short Passages

Passage one 1-5 BCCCC
Passage two 1-5 BBCCC

Reading Skills

The thesis statement: Jeff Bezos believes that a successful entrepreneur should have a view of divine discontent. Furthermore, entrepreneurship and invention are closely coupled.

Academic Words in Use

1. annoyed   2. assigned   3. capture   4. virtual   5. male
6. affection   7. emissions   8. launched   9. normally   10. emphasizes
11. fascinated   12. industrial

Writing

Sample writing

My View on Entrepreneurship

Due to the increasing number of college graduates, it is difficult for students to find a job because of the fierce competition. Traditional jobs are fully employed. The government encourages graduates to start their own businesses.

I think entrepreneurship encouragement is a good policy. On the one hand, graduates can give full play to their talents. They can choose to do what they are good at, instead of carrying out plans and executing them in the office. Compared with command, self-employment is more creative.

It provides a free stage for people to give full rein to their abilities. On the other hand, self-management can bring a sense of satisfaction from scratch and make great achievements. People will enjoy the process and feel satisfied.

This feeling of being an entrepreneur is wonderful. People will be very enthusiastic and excited to accept challenges. The meaning of life is to make difference and self employment can make people feel that life is meaningful and wonderful.

Unit 8 Career Development

Video script

Apple CEO Cook Talking About Career Planning
NW: 343　GL: 5.9　AWL percentage: 2.11%　Duration: 2′50″　WPM: 123

- What's interesting is that it is now 25 years since you got your MBA and as part of your MBA experience, you were asked to write a 25-year-plan.

- I was.

- How did that work out for you?

(audience laughing)

- There was a professor… I think his name was Dr. Nailor. Does that sound right?

- Tom Nailor.

- Yeah, Tom Nailor. He was a great professor, and one of the things that he'd ask us to do was to write a 25-year-plan.

- Maybe some of you have had to do this. And, it was more of a personal plan. And, normally I would never remember this, but I was doing a commencement address a few years ago, and I was scrambling for some old things, and I found, in a box, this plan. And, this plan had turned yellow because of age, but I looked at it and I would say it was reasonably accurate for all of 18 to 24 months, after it was written.

And, it was nothing, there was nothing, not a single thing on it that was accurate post that, not a single thing.

(audience laughing)

- Zero!

- And, I think that the lesson there is, at least for me… maybe you guys will be different… maybe you have much more insight into what you may be doing, but for me the journey was not predictable at all.

- And, it goes sort of back to the Lincoln quote… the only thing I believe you can do is (to) prepare.

- And, the world is going to change many times. The environment is going to change many times.

- The companies that you work for are going to ebb and flow. You may wind up in the same company… you may not.

You may wind up in the same career… you may not.

You may wind up with the spouse you're married to now… you may not.

There are lots of things in your life. I hope that one doesn't change.

(audience laughing).

But, there are lots of things that change. And I think that you sort of have to have a north star.

And, stay with the north star and let those things go on about you,

and sort of find your… find your journey.

Understanding the video clip

1. Normally I would never remember this, but I was doing a <u>commencement address</u> a few years ago.
2. Maybe you have much more <u>insight</u> into what you may be doing, but for me the journey was not predictable at all.
3. It goes sort of back to the Lincoln quote… the only thing I believe you can do is (to) <u>prepare</u>.
4. The companies that you work for are going to <u>ebb and flow</u>.
5. Stay with <u>the north star</u> and let those things go on about you.

Further thoughts

Open-ended discussion

Banked Cloze

1-5 KLMIH   6-10 ADFEC

Long Passage

1-5 GHFFH   6-10 CDABE

Short Passages

Passage one 1-5 CBDBD

Passage two 1-5 BCCAD

Reading Skills

Words connecting ideas are: for example, especially, perhaps, add all of this up, yet

Academic Words in Use

1. fulfilment
2. educational
3. like-minded
4. cognitive
5. engine
6. switching
7. origins
8. recycling
9. features
10. fiercely
11. trigger
12. acquisition

Writing

Sample writing

On College Students' Career Planning

With the development of society, an increasing number of teenagers have opportunities to be educated. It is beneficial to our nation and society. However, problems of career planning arise with this phenomenon. More and more pressure on employment is exposed to college students. So a lot of colleges have paid more attention to college students' career planning. It seems that this phenomenon is becoming a trend.

Career planning does not guarantee that all the problems, difficulties, or decision-making situations that you face in the future will be solved or made any easier. No formula can be given to do that. But career planning should be able to help you to approach and cope better with new problems, such as deciding whether to enter educational or training programs, deciding whether to change jobs, and analyzing the difficulties you are having with a situation or a person.

Career planning is a never-ending process that continues from one stage to another. Every individual wants to grow and develop in the workplace continuously. Having a clear career plan will not only strengthen your sense of faith, it will also motivate you to move forward. Only by making a good career plan can one stick to his/her goals and ultimately achieve success.